MW01628216

A PROFESSIONAL SOURCEBOOK AND PRACTICAL GUIDE TO

GARDEN DESIGN

A PROFESSIONAL SOURCEBOOK AND PRACTICAL GUIDE TO

GARDEN DESIGN

How to create a contemporary outdoor living space

Creative ideas for constructing and transforming your garden, with expert advice on flooring, surfaces, walls, construction, furniture, ornamental features and decorative items, shown in over 600 beautiful photographs

JOAN CLIFTON

Author's Acknowledgements
I would like to thank all the garden owners and designers who contributed to this book, for their generosity, hospitality, time and co-operation and for allowing their privacy to be invaded. Their energy and creativity sparkles throughout their accomplishments.

My admiration and thanks go to the project contributors who pulled out all the stops to devise and make original and stimulating features.

I owe immense gratitude to Jo Whitworth and Steven Wooster for their lovely photographs, painstaking attention to detail and fortitude during long, and occasionally uncomfortable, sorties into British weather.

I am indebted to Caroline Davison and give special thanks for her energy, enduring support, patience and unfailing ability to keep everything on track.

Thanks also to my family and friends for tolerating bouts of mental and physical absence, and especially to John Raffin for his infinite humour and support.

This edition published by Hermes House, an imprint of Anness Publishing Ltd, Hermes House, 88-89 Blackfriars Road, London SE1 8HA
tel. 020 7401 2077; fax 020 7633 9499
www.hermeshouse.com; www.annesspublishing.com

If you like the images in this book and would like to investigate using them for publishing, promotions or advertising, please visit our website www.practicalpictures.com for more information.

Previously published in two separate volumes: *Garden Elements* and *Stone, Wood, Glass and Steel*.

Publisher Joanna Lorenz
Editorial Director Helen Sudell
Executive Editor Caroline Davison
Designers Larraine Shamwana, Louise Clements
Jacket Designer Simon Daley
Photographers Jo Whitworth, Steven Wooster
Production Controller Wendy Lawson
Editorial Reader Hayley Kerr
Stylist Gilly Love

ETHICAL TRADING POLICY
Because of our ongoing ecological investment programme, you, as our customer, can have the pleasure and reassurance of knowing that a tree is being cultivated on your behalf to naturally replace the materials used to make the book you are holding. For further information about this scheme, go to www.annesspublishing.com/trees

Jacket back flap, bottom right: Chelsea Flower Show 2002 "Elevation" Designers: Eric de Maeijere & Jane Hudson

Contents

introduction

Think of a garden as a very special kind of theatre. The trees and shrubs juxtaposed with walls, fences and paving make up the scenery, the plants are the actors, while the furniture and other features are the props.

A garden involves the interaction of plants with inanimate objects and forms. It can be purely a plant collection, an array of forms, textures and colours, all vying for attention. Plants change shape through the seasons; they increase in size; they produce flowers, fruits and seeds; finally their leaves change colour and fall. Perennials die down in winter, deciduous trees and shrubs sustain a framework throughout the year, while evergreens are constant features.

However, in order for gardens to be shown to their best advantage, plants need focus to emphasize their qualities. If you want a visually effective garden that will stimulate the intellect, permeate ambience and flair or even reveal a sense of humour, it is essential to consider the supporting elements. This type of garden has structure and form; it reflects the nature and architecture of its surroundings and includes features that give character and interest throughout the year.

This book examines the structural and decorative elements that provide a framework and focus in the garden. It takes you through the basics of form, shape and pattern, then explores the sensual qualities of colour, texture and sound, in the context of international styles, both contemporary and traditional. We visit grand, classical gardens with a view to learning new ways to adapt formal fashions from the past; we travel to the Mediterranean to find a relaxed style to reflect current informal tastes and the naturalist approach of the Japanese gardening tradition is opened up to reveal connections with organic and elemental philosophies for the 21st century. From rose-strewn cottage retreats to rugged Atlantic coasts, you will find a plethora of images to stimulate ideas for your own garden.

All the familiar elements or building blocks, suitable for the range of different gardening styles, are then explored. A wide variety of hard landscaping details, including paving, steps, bridges and tiling, are detailed in their various settings, and construction materials are described according to their suitability for each purpose. You will find lots of ways to bring water into the garden, with features varying from the formal to the bizarre. Different styles of furniture and planters are placed in context to help you create distinctive sitting spaces.

We aim to excite your interest in contemporary sculpture by revealing the work of talented artists, while an inspiring collection of projects, ranging from simple painting to more challenging joinery, will tempt you to have a go yourself.

Above: **Terracotta floor tiles and steps provide a mellow background for this courtyard in which mature palms, olives and bananas are thriving.**

Below right: **Clipped balls of green santolina form an interesting geometric pattern which is reinforced at the rear by tall "lollipop" standard trees.**

Above left: **Sweeping beds of perennials and a stone cottage smothered with climbers epitomize the charms of a romantic garden. A vibrant colour scheme combines the red tones of *Helenium* 'Moerheim Beauty' and *Lilium bulbiferum*.**

Opposite: **In hot sunny climates, pergolas can create welcome shade while giving support to a wide variety of fruiting and flowering climbers.**

Plants, hard landscaping and other decorative features all contribute an element of mass to a garden. The organization of these elements into a cohesive form will control the garden's balance and character.

form and shape

The form of objects is defined by lines and the brain is conditioned to perceive these lines in certain ways, depending upon their arrangement. Parallel lines, whether straight or curved, are orderly and therefore feel calming; cross them diagonally with another set of lines, and they become chaotic. Visual weight plays a part in this balancing act too. Placing a shape such as a square or circle at one end of the parallel lines focuses the eye on this point; duplicate the shape at the other end of the lines and the result is an equalization that creates a visual balance.

The shape of an object depends partly on its function and partly on the material from which it is made. Linear shapes, straight or curved, can be made from timber and steel or by cutting the material into sections, complex designs for furniture and trellis can be created. Clay can be moulded into bricks and tiles, or thrown on a wheel to make a flowerpot.

The circle, square and triangle are the primary shapes from which all other forms derive, and each has different characteristics. In plan view, a circle can create a central feature in a formal

Above left: **This stone ball is being drawn back into the earth by inquisitive ivy.**

Above centre: **A ball stands as a sentinel in the path, yet draws the eye to the stones on the left.**

Above right: **A steel spiral draws the eye upwards, giving an illusion of vertical movement.**

Opposite: **The strength of these evergreen shapes, emphasized by winter frost, provides year-round form and structure.**

layout, perhaps as a low wall or hedge to enclose a fountain, pool or statue. It can be set out as a linear detail in overlapping groups for an asymmetric paving design. Set on its side, the circle could form an opening for a vista through a wall or hedge. Pulled up, the circle becomes a cylinder, which might be seen as a structural column or as a planting container.

When the circle is massed up, it becomes a sphere; this can be set in concrete or woven in willow to make a sculptural feature. Spheres made from stone, timber or metal can be finials for gateposts or obelisks. Plants, such as box (*Buxus*) and lavender, can also be formed into spheres. The classic "lollipop" bay tree is a sphere on top of a tall stem.

The square, composed of straight parallel lines meeting at right angles, is the basis of formal design. It can contain a garden room with walls, or a parterre with hedges; it will enclose a central area to set off a feature or create a series of spaces.

The triangle's major role in the garden is in the vertical plane. Combined with a circle, it can be drawn up into a cone, which makes an excellent form on which to train climbers. It can be made from wirework or steel, which combine strength with visual lightness, or, for a more rustic effect, willow or timber. The cone is also a simple form for box or yew (*Taxus baccata*) topiary.

From the cone comes the spiral; this can be cut from solid plant material as topiary, or make up part of the construction of a climbing frame. Returned to the flat plane, a spiral can create a channel for a water feature, be formed in tiles for a mosaic or raked into pebbles for a Japanese theme.

Opposite (top): **The rectilinear form of this pool has been cleverly staggered both vertically and horizontally from the timber deck on which it is constructed. Energetic, blade-like planting creates a dramatic contrast to the smooth plane of water.**

Opposite (bottom): **The use of plants in an architectural capacity is shown clearly in this textural design. A narrow flight of stone steps is driven upwards by the trunks of tall palm trees, their dramatic fronds echoed by the spiky foliage of yuccas and cordylines.**

Top left: **The strongly directional form of this wrought-iron gate points the way to a group of soaring, columnar cypress trees in the distance. Tall bastions of closely clipped yew support the vertical theme, by lining the route towards them.**

Centre left (top): **Massed topiary with layers of clipped balls, wedges and pyramids shows the variety of forms that can be created from a single plant.**

Centre left (bottom): **The spiral represents an energetic life force, and this detail of a woven willow fence seems to spin like a newly lit firework.**

Bottom left: **Vertical blue spirals provide a dramatic contrast in form and colour to the low, tightly clipped santolina balls.**

Above right: **The vertical axis of the silver birch is crossed by the dark slate bench. The eye is drawn through by a succession of low green plant balls.**

Right: **An old yew tree has been tackled courageously to create a dramatic spiral.**

Patterns occur everywhere in nature, from the organization of leaves and petals to the striation of minerals in rock. They are the inspiration behind all our design theories.

pattern

Patterns comprise groups of marks arranged together in such a way that they create a picture. Variations in the shape and composition of the marks can result in endless permutations of pattern and design, whether they be geometric, abstract or figurative. These marks are usually defined as lines: wavy or straight, formed in circles or squares, arranged in groups of stripes, and set on the vertical, horizontal or diagonal.

Circles can be drawn out into a spiral – one of the fundamental life forces representing the energy of underground watercourses and the unfurling of fern fronds. The spiral formation of a snail shell has a mathematical formula that is repeated identically in all molluscs, and this shape occurs again and again throughout nature.

The complex patterns found on flower petals sometimes utilize dots and spots that serve to guide insects towards the pollen held on the stamens of flowers, rather like an airport runway. Used as part of a paving pattern, these patterns can perform a similar

Above left: **Round balls of bright green grasses contrast sharply with a glass "mulch".**

Above centre: **Patterns can occur naturally, as this *Melianthus major* leaf shows (top), or on manmade objects such as this piece of carved timber (bottom).**

Above right: **A pattern of stars within squares is emphasized by tall conical shapes.**

Opposite: **A parterre provides an opportunity to explore pattern.**

function by leading the eye towards a particular focal point or perhaps by emphasizing the way along a path.

Pattern in all its exciting variety may be used in hard landscaping in a number of different ways. Paving provides one of the most versatile opportunities. Suitable components are numerous, and the manner of laying further extends their potential impact. Bricks may be laid lengthways or on end, in straight lines, at right angles or in zigzag formation, each style resulting in a totally different visual effect. The incorporation of an additional element, such as slate, can form an edging border or serve to separate different pattern layouts.

Cobbles and pebbles are available in a wide range of sizes and shapes, including round, oval and square. Neutral colours from whites to blacks are cool and contemporary, and should be combined subtly to define the pattern. Cobbles and pebbles are also extremely useful where curved shapes are involved, and work effectively for centrepieces and pond surrounds. Pebbles used in a combination of colours also lend themselves to complex figurative designs where a distinctive focal point is required.

Exotic and complex patterns are often created with coloured glazed tiles, either cut into small pieces in order to make a mosaic, or left whole for larger-scale effects. Their fragility and poor wearing qualities make them most suitable for details on walls, risers of steps or tabletops and sculptural features. Our Mosaic Table project on page 198–201 may well stimulate you in this direction.

Top left: **An innovative archway made from a combination of willow and hazel creates a dramatic passageway to the woodland beyond.**

Below left: **Snaking spirals of small grey santolinas connect the domed mounds and lollipop standards of the topiary.**

Below: **This water feature was designed with great foresight in 1928. White railings, curved to enforce the visual gradient, frame successive flights of steps. The trunks of the silver birches reinforce the upward motion of the design and echo the rails, while the delicate foliage adds a sense of lightness.**

Bottom left: **Rectangular bands of violas contrast with narrow strips of green box hedging.**

Bottom centre: **The progression of a curved pathway between beds of thyme is indicated by a succession of Roman numerals which are set in circles amidst round stones.**

Bottom right: **Wrought-iron gates provide an excellent opportunity to contrast visual pattern with its adjacent planting. The spirals are a particularly popular choice among blacksmiths, and have an earthy resonance because their shape resembles that of unfurling plant tendrils.**

Colour is sensual; it evokes moods and creates atmosphere. It can generate feelings of tranquillity and contemplation, or it can produce drama and excitement.

colour

Colour can be used for instant makeover effects. Tired fences, decorative structures and furniture can be brought back to life with a coat of one of the new outdoor paints. Decorate dingy walls in shades of pale yellow to reflect light, or use ochre tints in a bright area to create a Mediterranean feeling. By choosing a shade like bright blue or deep purple for timber or metal furniture, you can create dramatic contrasts in a contemporary setting.

You can create an integrated colour scheme with toning shades to pull together disparate elements. Fences could be pale grey-green, with a pergola or arch in a deeper toning green. A shed could reflect the scheme by being painted in stripes of both colours or having window and door details picked out in one.

To unify a group of miscellaneous pots, paint them in a themed design like those in our project on page 208–209. Old watering cans and tin canisters can be given a new look, and old painted tools can be arranged together to make a colourful "found sculpture".

Above left: **The blue glaze of this stoneware pot contrasts with the red pelargonium.**

Above centre: **This Moroccan blue wall is criss-crossed with scrambling bougainvillaea.**

Above right: **The blue walls and pool edge create a rich foil for yellow pots and exotic plants.**

Opposite: **Rectangles of deep red plastic create a vibrantly hot theme, reinforced by brilliant orange flowers.**

Below: **The choice of pale blue paint gives this bench and planter a sophisticated air. It is complemented perfectly by the white standard rose and underplanting of petunias.**

Bottom: **The aged effect of peeling, pale blue paint combines beautifully with the pale terracotta of this Mediterranean urn.**

Instead of plain earthenware containers, plant bright pots for an exotic display on a terrace. Tiles and mosaics bring reflective glints as well as rich textures; use them on floors or on the surface of tables, to enliven old pots or as inlaid features in a wall.

Glass and acrylic plastic are exciting materials, having qualities of light transmission and colour absorption. They can be used to create water features or mobiles, or as translucent panels can be set into walls to give light without losing privacy.

Are you cool or are you hot? Make the effect you want to achieve by selecting the appropriate group of colours. Searing magenta and hot pinks, deep azures and glowing purples all suggest hot climates, cloudless skies and blazing sunshine. They are effective if you live in a sun-soaked southern environment, surrounded by elaborate tropical flowers with colourful birds and insects. These brilliant colours are wonderful if you want to be reminded of tropical holidays all year round.

On the other hand, bright colours can look uncomfortable in northern light under steel-grey skies. It is here that the pale shades come into their own; soft and elegant, they complement and support. Lovat greens and pewter greys give subtle contrast to foliage, while delicate lilacs and warm blues pick up the tones of flowers in the red/blue spectrum. They also work well in shady areas, glowing through and reflecting the available light.

The neutrals are cool and sophisticated. They are natural, with earth tones of clay and stone, pale creams through to soft browns. The deeper shades of grey and black, amber and terracotta strengthen the theme. Think of adobe houses in New Mexico, teak stilt houses in Thailand and stone houses in the Cotswolds. Each location is distinctive, but connecting them is the use of indigenous materials to create subtle and complementary buildings.

Above: **Pale blue furniture sits very comfortably among garden foliage. This subtly exotic scene is enhanced by the intelligent choice of lime-green fabrics for the cushions and parasol.**

Opposite (bottom right): **The soft mauve-blue of this fine wirework spiral makes a clever visual statement nestling among intense blue monkshoods and pale pink campanulas.**

The texture of an item suggests so much potential sensuality. From the smoothness of sea-washed pebbles to the coarseness of weathered stonework, texture brings a sensory dimension to the garden.

texture

Although touch is not absolutely essential to appreciate the qualities of texture, when your eye alights on an interesting surface, it is almost impossible to restrain yourself from reaching out to touch. How frustrating to find a notice beside a sculpture forbidding touch. It is like being denied the chance to experience the thoughts and the feelings of the artist.

Materials change entirely in texture and character, depending on the surface treatment that is applied. There is a world of difference between rough-sawn timber and carefully planed bespoke trelliswork. The smooth, sanded finish of an oak seat also reveals the high quality of the timber. When softwoods are painted, the natural grain is lost to view and the surface becomes smooth. If it is treated with a tinted stain, however, the grain and texture will still show through.

Granite, a massively hard and heavy rock, appears unyielding and aggressive when highly polished, but if the surface is given a lightly hammered treatment, it looks much softer.

Above: **A variety of different textures including rusting metal washers (top left); a spiral of crushed windscreen glass (top centre); a lichen-covered brick wall (top right); rough-sawn timber (bottom left); glass pebbles and deeply ridged mollusc shells (bottom centre); smooth pebbles (bottom right).**

Opposite: **An inventive mosaic of blue, glazed tile fragments highlights this maritime garden of smooth, sea-washed stones and spiky planting.**

Manufacturing processes can also change the texture and performance of the finished product. Stock building bricks are rough and absorbent, while engineering bricks feel hard, with a shiny resilience to water and frost. Similarly, hand-made terracotta pots feel pleasantly grainy, textured and mellow, while factory-moulded versions are shiny, with a rather dull appearance.

The same change can be seen and felt in metals. When iron is cast in a mould, the result is a heavy and lifeless article. Real wrought iron, a rare beast now, is pulled and hammered after heating and can be used to make decorative pieces of extreme delicacy.

Mild steel is also fashioned in this way, but does not possess the same flexible qualities or resistance to rust. However, a rusty surface has an attractively rustic texture which should be considered for an informal situation, looking very much at home among garden plants. Bright and reflective, stainless steel is smooth and hard. It has rust-resistant qualities and permits the clean, strong lines demanded by contemporary designers.

The malleable properties of soft lead sheet make it suitable for applied decoration and finishing, while cast lead is hard and less bendable. Zinc has similar qualities, although its appearance is initially bright. Steel may be dipped in liquid zinc for rust-proofing.

Clearly, the texture of materials chosen for the garden will determine its character and atmosphere. Shiny, hard surfaces are formal and metropolitan whereas rough finishes suggest a more casual feeling.

Opposite and centre left (bottom): **Slate can be used to evoke imaginary river beds and create strong sculptural effects.**

Top left: **Glass aggregate creates a reflective infill between beds.**

Above: **Shiny surfaces are smooth and bring reflective qualities to the garden.**

Top right: **Deeply veined hostas soften the edge of a rocky pool.**

Centre right: **Weathered wood has an interesting texture.**

Bottom right: **Grey and golden lichens adorn this stone finial.**

Below: **Tiny saxifrages contrast with the hard pebbles and the spiky pinks (*Dianthus*).**

Centre left (top): **A smooth ball contrasts with rough timber, fine gravel and glaucous foliage.**

Poplar leaves rattling in the wind, the sound of rustling bamboos, the splash of a fountain, the familiar chirp of singing birds – these are just some of the myriad sounds to discover and create in the garden.

sound

Because sound is invisible, it is usually overlooked as a dimension of garden design, but, used creatively, it can enhance and benefit your surroundings. A highly effective way of introducing sound is with water, which can be one of the most relaxing and satisfying sounds in the world. There is something very soothing about the gentle bubbling and flowing of moving water. It does need to be introduced thoughtfully, however: a vigorous splashing can be overwhelming, while at the other end of the scale tiny drips and trickles may become a trifle irritating. So remember to choose your water feature with care, especially if you have a small garden in which every splish and splash can be heard.

The presence of water will attract birds to the garden, so make sure that there are some shallow places for them to drink and bathe; these need to be safe from the attentions of local cats. The sound of birdsong gives us a real contact with the natural world and is a tremendous antidote to city stresses. To be woken in the morning by

Above left: **The sound of water splashing on to stones is both refreshing and enlivening.**

Above centre: **The "frothy" sound of this fountain suits the little floating figure.**

Above right: **Birds bring life and amusement to a garden; this frolicking tit is enjoying an exuberant toilette.**

Opposite: **Suspended slivers of carved Welsh slate combine sound with sculptural effect.**

the dawn chorus is something even town dwellers can enjoy, and it is comforting to hear the birds' evening song at dusk. If you want to attract birds all year round, remember to feed them regularly, especially in winter, when they are struggling against frozen ground and water, as well as the absence of insects and other natural foods.

Attention to the needs of wildlife in the garden can reap unexpected rewards for the ear. A snuffling and shuffling family of hedgehogs will be delighted by offerings of cat food. The buzzing of bumble bees will accompany a mass of lavender and rosemary bushes. A squirrel, munching its way through a tree of green almonds, makes a spectacular noise, though not one that is always welcome!

Remember how much fun it was as a child to run and scuffle through a pile of fallen leaves in the woods? Leaves, tinder dry on the ground in the autumn, or fresh and shining on a branch in spring, offer a whole library of wonderful sounds. Even the slightest breeze will provoke evocative rustlings, while a good wind can produce howlings and rattlings worthy of ghost stories. Plant trees with sound in mind. Eucalyptus, in particular, makes a spectacular noise, and if the main trunk is stopped a little above head level, it will develop a wonderful canopy of branches to suit even a small garden. Bamboos and tall grasses situated by a path also release lovely rustlings as you brush past.

Capitalize on the winds and breezes, and remember that a wind chime hung in a doorway or a mobile suspended from a tree branch can add another interesting sound dimension.

Opposite (top): **A lively fountain jet cascades over its bowl to trickle down to the pool below.**

Opposite (bottom): **A wonderfully textured Japanese feature has been created from an old cider press. The bamboo spout releases water, which trickles quietly on to the pebbles below.**

Left: **Wind chimes combine sweet sound with style.**

Below: **Still waters run deep, but not silent. Croaking frogs lurk around the pond edge and fish flap their tails on the surface.**

the styles

Style is a matter of personality, of understanding who you are. It is about character, not fashion; about creativity, not cost. The style of your garden is created by the way you see, feel and live. All your experiences affect your personality, and your garden will be a reflection of these influences.

In order to help you recognize and create a personal garden style, we have analysed the most significant aspects you need to consider. References are taken from history, showing how fashions over the centuries still influence ideas today.

Appropriate decorative items are suggested to complement the various looks, from rustic country garden to chic city terrace. From the guidelines offered, you will be able to piece together all the elements to realize your unique vision.

Plants, too, have their own individual, horticultural personalities, and we help you to understand the difference choosing the right plants will have on your garden. A thoughtful co-ordination of plants and the hard elements of landscaping will make your garden design a success.

Your geographical location will have a profound effect on your garden, from the point of view of both landscape and climate. We show you how to recognize the styles that will work best in your particular environment.

Cultural differences influence us when travelling, when watching films and when reading books. We look at important gardening styles from around the world, featuring gardens that are up to date with the increasingly popular minimalist style.

Opposite (top): **A low, pale-coloured wall surrounds a cool, Zen-inspired courtyard, paved with soft grey slate and creamy gravel. A simple planting of papyrus grasses and moss around the little pond is all that is needed to complete the sense of calm and tranquillity.**

Opposite (centre): **Vertical tree trunks and steel spirals emphasize the directional progression of the path in this formal town garden.**

Opposite (bottom): **Brilliant scarlet poppies pierce the early morning mist which so often envelops seaside gardens.**

Left: **A narrow channel of water bisects a path connecting two low fountains, creating a calming division between the mounds of exotic planting which surround it in this Mediterranean garden.**

formal

Garden design can be traced back to the Egyptians, but the landmark period of the Italian Renaissance in the 15th century has influenced garden design until the present day. Classical form has been translated through the centuries, encompassing fashions right up to the contemporary designs emerging in the new millennium.

Left: **Imposing classical Italian terracotta pots bring textural contrast, scale and presence to this formal parterre composed of low green box hedging.**

Below: **These symmetrical borders are emphasized by pairs of standard trees which are underplanted with clipped box. Elegant box pyramids punctuate the end of each narrow canal.**

The strictly rectilinear design is reinforced by the square-cut underplanting and horizontally banded background wall. The white wild boar acts as a focal point for the arrangement.

Centuries ago, powerful landowners commissioned the finest architects and landscapers to create their estates. Labour was plentiful and cheap, and technical skills in building were being developed, so it was possible to construct domains of staggering complexity and classical grandeur, which were imitated in successive centuries throughout Europe.

One only has to consider the vast scale of Versailles outside Paris, in France, with its huge earth-moving achievements, and the management and control of water in canals and fountains, to appreciate the skills and philosophies of its creator, Le Nôtre, which remain with us as inspiration today. The practice of clipping hundreds of topiaries and the transfer of dozens of palms and exotics in and out of the orangery at each turn of the seasons is still faithfully preserved.

The vastness of such estates demanded a supreme understanding of scale and proportion. Areas of land were divided by paths, avenues and canals; long flights of steps graced changes in level. These devices served to create the balance and form of the overall plan. The vistas

thus created formed long views through to statues and fountains, and provided elegant thoroughfares for promenading and games.

The smaller compartments formed between these paths were bordered by hedges of yew (*Taxus baccata*) and hornbeam (*Carpinus*) to emphasize their shape and containment. They are the forerunners to our current conception of the garden room. An exceptionally effective way to treat the traditional long, narrow plot is to divide it up into different areas, each one hidden from the next. In this way, the garden is revealed gradually as you pass through it, providing surprises and complete changes of look in a relatively small area. Even a tiny yard can be contained effectively in one single theme.

Formal gardens are perfectly suited to the metropolitan environment in which so many of us live. The constraints of small spaces set among densely packed houses and apartments can be exploited, because the presence of high walls and surrounding buildings gives privacy to your domain. The need for clarity among so many conflicting influences makes an ordered garden a calming solution.

Left: **Rhythmic pairs of trees create a rectilinear progression that crosses through horizontal canals. The clean trunks and square-cut box send a clear structural message in this contemporary garden.**

Above: **A handsome bench made from black slate rests on paving of black engineering bricks. The neatly clipped balls of box and helxine serve to offset the predominance of rectangular shapes.**

The parterre, a favourite planting device in the 17th century, is now finding horticultural favour again today. Within compartments enclosed by high screening, low hedges of box (*Buxus*) and aromatic herbs were laid out in curving or straight geometric patterns, known as knot gardens. If this seems daunting, make a simple arrangement of four compartments set in squares formed by low hedging. At the central point between them, set a focal point such as an urn, a sundial or a fountain.

In spring, bulbs provide an ideal infill within the squares. The combination of dark green box and white tulips is magical, while black tulips within silver-grey santolinas are sheer sophistication. In summer, in a sunny situation, you might choose feathery leaved cosmos, with huge white or carmine flowers. In town, shade is more likely, so white, scented tobacco plants (*Nicotiana*) or white busy Lizzies (*Impatiens*) would be perfect. Winter brings the possibility of cyclamen or heather to complete the planting cycle. This is an effective way to ring in the seasonal changes in a small garden, while maintaining the evergreen backbone and structure of the design. For a final

Above left: **Low yew hedging and standard trees draw one inexorably towards a distant Gothic folly.**

Left: **Rectangular beds of grey santolinas, which have been clipped into tight balls, alternate with flat planes of lavender. The sophisticated and slightly surreal effect of the topiary in this parterre is further emphasized by the stocky little cones of box that sit at the corners of the low surrounding hedges.**

touch, the urn may be planted with a clipped evergreen, such as holly (*Ilex*), bay (*Laurus nobilis*) or box, or it may reflect the flower scheme of the parterre.

Topiary, or the art of training plants into shapes, has gone in and out of fashion since Roman times. It is currently seeing a fervent renaissance, and no self-respecting house in

London, for example, would be without at least a pair of lollipop bays set in Versailles planters at the entrance door. Architectural shapes like cones, balls and spirals always look smart and elegant, and will work well in both traditional and contemporary schemes.

Suitable plant subjects include the old favourites of box, yew (*Taxus baccata*) and bay, but many other shrubs and trees can also be used. Rosemary (*Rosmarinus*) and lavender (*Lavandula*) make good spheres; pyracanthas can be trained into shapes against walls; and even rustic hawthorn (*Crataegus*) can be given a sophisticated appearance by clipping.

Many familiar species take on a totally new character when pruned formally. Camellias and azaleas can be grown as hedges and trimmed closely with secateurs (hand pruners) in the

Above: **A circular parterre is divided into equal segments which are bordered by box hedging and focused at the centre by an elegant statue. This design formalizes the mixed groups of herbs making up the infill planting.**

Above right: **The segments of the parterre are focused at the centre by box cones. The mono species infill planting of lavender and sage has a calming effect.**

Right: **Yew obelisks lead to brick pillars and a summerhouse.**

Left: **Successive pairs of *Robinia pseudoacacia* create a rhythmic progression down this avenue.**

Below: **A graceful statue is framed by a tall beech hedge and a seasonal underplanting of brilliantly contrasting yellow wallflowers (*Erysimum*).**

Japanese manner, while box and pines (*Pinus*), Japanese holly (*Ilex crenata*) and common myrtle (*Myrtus communis*), spruce (*Picea*) and fir trees (*Abies*) can all be given the cloud topiary treatment revealed in our project on page 140–143.

Wirework frames are readily available to help you to shape and train your project. Wire is an exciting, flexible material that can be made into a host of other objects such as furniture, obelisks and trelliswork as well as training frames for plants. The latter can be used to create instant topiary effects from climbing plants such as evergreen ivy (*Hedera*) in its numerous varieties or, in warm climates, the creeping fig, *Ficus pumila*.

Opposite (bottom right): **A classical terracotta urn makes a fitting statement before a rise of steps.**

Below: **A gambolling water lover makes an amusing feature.**

Bottom: **Formal containers make dramatic focal points.**

By training a flowering climber such as clematis or passionflower on to a shape such as a cone, it is possible to tame the unruliness of their natural habit while showing off the individual blooms to their full advantage. Combinations of clematis, such as pure white *Clematis* 'Marie Boisselot' with soft mauve *C.* x 'Lasurstern' are most effective, while the silvery seed heads of some of the species such as *C. tangutica* mean that they stay beautiful long after flowering has ceased.

Above: **Drama is created by a majestic pediment and a balustrade surmounting a steep progression of stone steps. The borders of box and bergenia that edge the flight of steps serve to emphasize the curving upward lines.**

The introduction of water into a formal garden creates a significant dynamic, contrasting with the planting scheme, while enforcing the rhythm of the overall design. Water introduces light and life, reflecting sunlight and mirror images of surrounding trees and objects. A still pool is like a quiet pause, provoking a tranquil and thoughtful ambience while the introduction of a fountain or rill brings life with dancing movement and sound.

Formal pools may be at ground level or raised up but are always defined by a border of solid material that continues the hard landscaping theme. A ground level pool is excavated from the earth and lined with butyl sheeting or a purpose-made fibreglass shell. This is held in place and finished by a border of stone slabs, paving blocks or bricks.

An above-ground pool is contained within low walls that can be constructed of natural stone, brick or rendered concrete with an appropriate stone or tile capping. If the walls are built from any kind of block material, the interior should be waterproofed and sealed with a liner. Alternatively it might be completely constructed with poured concrete moulded within a formwork of shuttering. Concrete must be sealed with an appropriate waterproofing system or, more elegantly, finished with deep-toned glazed ceramic tiles.

Above: **A path connects a low stone pool to the balustrade beyond. The clothing of pink rambling roses makes the enchanting, white water lilies look even more romantic.**

Top centre: **A grand tier of waterfalls completes this neo-classical design. The construction of riven stone and slates gives it a sense of drama and power to complement the villa and gateway.**

To increase the visual effect of a formal pool, the introduction of a fountain can produce glamorous effects ranging from the subtle to the flamboyant. Depending upon the power of the pump, complex combinations of jets, sprays and cascades can be achieved, but often, the simplest ideas work best. A group of bubble jets that gently break the surface will transform

the impression of a still pool without causing a surfeit of noise or distraction. Alternatively a single jet can be combined with an object like a globe or a millstone to add an architectural dimension. However, if the intention is to create high drama, a large installation might incorporate tall jets rising and falling to different heights or a cascade over an abstract sculpture.

Wall fountains are a good choice where space is limited, and this is an area where a self-contained design can be employed. However, you can have fun designing your own. A mask provides the opportunity for a spout to emerge from its mouth. Water collects in a bowl below for circulation. The scale can vary and the force of water adapted to suit the design.

For a bigger splash, create a cascade. Instead of a spout in the wall, create a horizontal slot, 1–2m (3–6ft) wide, from which water can crash in one continuous surge. This will obviously need professional installation and a special site, preferably one with plenty of space in an area with changing levels.

Lighting alters the visual effect of water at night immeasurably, and is especially effective when the feature is close to the house, or a terrace where it can easily be seen. Lights installed in the base or side walls of the pool during construction will serve especially well to focus on any sculptural features within the design. The effects of sunlight on water often result in unsightly build up of algae, so to prevent water stagnation, a pumped filtration system can be incorporated at the same time. Attention to safety is a must for all electrical installations outside and a qualified professional should carry out the work.

Above: **A low-powered jet disturbs the surface of a rectangular pool bordered by flat stone slabs. The bronze cats sits wistfully, hoping for an imaginary goldfish.**

Centre (bottom): **The boundary of standard-trained trees, which appear to have to cope with a permanently prevailing wind, give a sense of containment and shelter to this stone-walled pool.**

romantic

Borders bursting with flowers of all sizes and colours, rambling roses spilling over a wall, and chickens wandering in a potager filled with succulent vegetables: these are the images of country living. Whether in town or country, you can create a romantic idyll in which to lose yourself among the perfumes and flavours of the good life.

Left: **A stone-paved seating area, softly framed by cascading laburnum and informal groups of flowering perennials, epitomizes the romantic country style.**

Romance suggests softness, abundance and fluidity. Rather than control the garden rigidly, create differently themed areas with informal links between them.

Of all the flowers, roses epitomize romance, and of all the roses, the old varieties, with their voluptuous, evocatively scented blooms, are the ultimate in sensual beauty. You can create a special rose garden to indulge yourself in all the gorgeous forms of flower. Groups that include Bourbon and Gallica roses with names like 'Boule de Neige', 'Cardinal Richelieu' and 'Fantin Latour' are just so mouth-watering that they become irresistible. Colours from rich cream, through sugar-almond pink to the deepest purple, with perfumes to match, tempt you further into their trap. Give them lovely silver and blue companion planting to create seductive combinations that will extend the effect throughout the seasons.

In another area, make a garden focused on water. If there is a boundary wall, a simple spout through a lion's-head mask can trickle into a lead cistern below. In a more central position, create a round pool with a fountain spraying water droplets on to floating waterlilies (*Nymphaea*). For a stunning combination of deep blue and sulphur yellow, encircle it with a hedge of lavender surrounded by lady's mantle (*Alchemilla mollis*).

Use pathways to invite discovery and allow them to meander between garden spaces. Soft bricks, old stones and cobbles all possess the required mellowness, blending sympathetically with flowers and foliage. In a wild area, where paving is inappropriate, mow a path through meadow grass. For spring, plant drifts of daffodils (*Narcissus*) and early bulbs, extending the colour from summer to autumn with successive sowings of wild flower seeds.

Hidden pathways suggest mysterious journeys. Create a tunnel of Japanese wisteria to allow the pendulous blooms to show to full advantage, or experiment with mixed honeysuckles (*Lonicera*) to create successive flowering and scent throughout the summer.

The romantic garden calls for a sensitive touch with furniture. It should be decorative as well as functional, making a creative contribution to the garden. Try to find interesting shapes that demonstrate delicacy or informality. The 18th and 19th centuries offer many romantic source references for furniture, with designs ranging from the classical to the fantastical. *Faux* rustic styles of furniture were popular at the turn of the last century, and can be suitable, made in either rough timber or hazelwood.

Fine wrought-iron and wirework chairs will combine sympathetically with soft planting schemes, and look fresh and

original when painted in new colours; the colours used in our mosaic project on page 198–201 are soothing and subtle.

Painted softwood furniture comes into its own when the colour picks up on the flower theme; go for red-toned blues and grey-greens, which are good foils, or opt for the purity of white when total simplicity is required.

A seating arbour makes a lovely feature – the perfect spot for secret trysts. It provides a wonderful excuse to grow perfumed climbers like roses, jasmine and honeysuckle, the theme of which can be continued along surrounding walls or trellis. It needs to be strong enough to carry the weight of the plants but still look delicate, so that it does not dominate the effect. The physical strength and visual lightness of wrought iron makes this a very suitable construction material; for an original look, paint it cream or blue-grey.

Opposite (left): **Folding canvas chairs are ideal for a hideaway.**

Opposite (centre): **A tiled-roof well echoes the house beyond. The profusion of purple clematis is another shared feature.**

Opposite (right): **Enjoy summer days on a rope-strung swing.**

Below: **Clematis-clad, bamboo trelliswork with symmetrical patterning creates a perfect backdrop to a border.**

The potager, with its mix of flowers, vegetables and herbs, is a romantic idyll to which many of us aspire. The taste of fresh produce that you have grown yourself and then picked will reward all your hard work and efforts at every delicious meal. There are so many unusual varieties now available that it is possible to bring new levels of style and flavour to your culinary endeavours in the kitchen garden. Ruby chard, purple curly kale and yellow tomatoes are just a few examples of the wide range of tantalizing colours and enticing textures now available to the vegetable designer.

When planning your space, experiment first on paper with different shapes and patterns. Straight lines make for efficient cultivation, but the plants do not need to be arranged in predictable rows. What works particularly well is a parterre arrangement, whereby you divide the area to be planted into four sections with a path running between them. Border each quarter with woody herbs clipped into little hedges; rosemary (*Rosmarinus*), thyme (*Thymus*) or sage (*Salvia*) would be suitable. Within them, arrange your planting design in radiating stripes or concentric circles, depending on the size and variety of subject.

If you have only a tiny space in which to develop a potager, it can be organized in a cartwheel form with triangles of herbs and salad leaves arranged between gravel spokes emanating from the central hub. Fill tall terracotta pots to overflowing with chives, marjoram and parsley, and group them in the corners. Utilize the vertical element with hazel tepees to support purple-podded peas, French beans (string beans) and decorative squashes, and form boundaries with trellises of runner beans (green beans) or blackberries.

Above: **A tepee of canes, densely clothed with climbing runner (green) beans, makes an attractive vertical statement among low-growing subjects.**

Left: **This potager at a French chateau is organized in an inventive parterre. It emanates sheer luxury and indulgence. The exaggerated use of mono species planting reveals the potential of form and texture in creating a design.**

Top right: **Vegetables that have strongly textured leaves, such as ruby chard and cardoon, are complemented well here by the red- and purple-leaved salad leaves. They are made even more effective by being planted in bold blocks.**

Right: **A simple ironwork walkway is transformed by a clothing of brilliantly coloured climbing nasturtiums and decorative gourds.**

Top: Metalwork arches clothed with pink and purple roses define a pathway bordered by blue veronica and lady's mantle.

Above: Salvias, alliums and larkspur (*Consolida*) float in mauve drifts punctuated by lime-green lady's mantle and red poppies. The result is a dreamily merging summer scene.

Top right: A trellis arbour filters sunlight on to an inventive path made from sawn timbers infilled with pebbles.

Top left: **Wirework chairs provide a vantage point from which to view these topiary peacocks.**

Main picture: **The unusual combination of flowering elder (*Sambucus*) with honeysuckle (*Lonicera*) acts as a frame for the farmland vista beyond.**

Top: **Swathes of *Geranium sylvaticum* barely leave enough space to walk through this romantic tunnel framed by an arch of trained apples.**

Above: **Pink climbing roses intertwine with fruiting vines over an old stone balustrade.**

mediterranean

The pungent scent of herbs on a hillside overlooking the sea; bright, whitewashed, stone houses reflecting the heat of the sun; al fresco meals in shady courtyards: the images of the Mediterranean are heady and sensuous, wild and evocative. Friends sharing food and conversation around a table; gravel on the ground and terracotta pots filled with rosemary – it is a formula for easy living, relaxed but considered, comfortable but chic.

Right: **This terracotta-tiled shelter, supported on pillars of twisted old timber, creates a temptingly shady retreat. The old cobble paving emphasizes its charming rusticity.**

To achieve the shabby-chic effect, appropriate materials for paving would be rough stone slabs, hewn not sanded, or rustic terracotta tiles. Gravel suits casual areas or infill between beds, where there is not too much foot traffic; cobbles are effective for curved designs and path details. These all give the required appearance of rugged earthiness and will, in addition, absorb and radiate the heat needed by indigenous plants.

Old stone walls have the textural qualities to make an ideal backdrop, but they are only feasible in certain areas. A versatile alternative is to construct surrounding walls from basic building blocks, then coat the surface with a plaster render and finish it in masonry paint. Umber and sienna tones are warm and welcoming, while grey-greens lend a cooler, restrained quality. As long as initial preparation has been good, maintenance is not

A successful Mediterranean-style garden needs to combine a feeling of untamed nature with a sophisticated sense of colour and form. The effect is informal, but it results from the considered selection and positioning of the constituent elements.

In cooler climates, a sun-soaked area would be the wisest choice for location, making a sheltered courtyard to contain the design and enable tender plants to thrive. In hot and exposed situations, the inclusion of an arbour or pergola covered with vines will provide welcome shade and contribute creatively to the ambience.

In garden design, the groundwork and perimeters hold the various parts of the theme together and control the overall look.

a problem: crumbling paintwork is all part of the look. However, if you favour Greek-island white, be prepared to paint every year.

Mediterranean living is convivial and relaxed. To enjoy it with family and friends you need to sit and, most importantly, to eat. The table is the focal point around which these activities take place, so choose one large enough to spread with bowls of tomatoes and figs, plates of salami and baskets of bread.

The classic French-style garden table is made with wrought iron, with matching chairs softened with cushions. Alternatively, a more sturdy approach could feature a timber base supporting a stone tabletop or one covered in zinc, with generous cane-work bucket chairs for a really long lunch.

Top left: **Simple terracotta pots, bursting with pelargoniums, line a stone terrace framed with shade trees and tall cypress.**

Centre left: **Vertical stone pillars echo the tree trunks beyond and frame an ironwork pergola. The rectilinear form is reinforced by the stone paving and low perimeter walls.**

Bottom left: **Sienna-toned walls make a subtle backdrop to show off plaster reliefs, marble statuary and granite pillars. A gate in the background reflects the interesting ironwork chairs.**

Right: **The base of this octagonal marble pool is lined with pebbles to make a centre-piece for this thoughtfully planned, geometric courtyard design, composed of combinations of black, grey and white. Interesting use of colour and shape are used to indicate direction towards the gate.**

Below: **A lemon tree epitomizes the character of a formal Mediterranean courtyard.**

Below right: **Random stonework is organized into narrow squares in this shady courtyard.**

The changes can be rung in quickly and inexpensively with different tablecloths and cushions. Provençal "Indienne" paisleys, for example, are stunning in combinations of blue, yellow and magenta; stripes are sophisticated in combinations of orange, green and taupe; and simple ginghams in pink or green are perennially fresh.

Terracotta pots must feature prominently in the Mediterranean, and the larger the better in order to cultivate the requisite clipped balls of box (*Buxus*) and bay (*Laurus nobilis*), or olives, lemons and figs if your climate permits. Containers tend to be most visually effective when used

A little café table and a couple of wirework chairs would be perfect for an al fresco breakfast or an intimate chat over a bottle of wine. Junk shops (thrift stores) are a good source of old rusting pieces, often salvaged from parks and restaurants, and there are some exquisite new ones to be tracked down at design shops and flower shows.

Decorative colour features throughout the Mediterranean garden. Informal furniture, whether made from metal or wood, can be painted according to your mood or prevailing trends. Again, this is one of those areas where gently peeling layers of successive paint choices can add immeasurably to the charm.

Below: **This wooden furniture has a rustic charm that is well suited to the terrace. A canopy of dense climbers provides shade.**

Bottom: **Smoky pink walls and steps in this courtyard soften the effect of intense sunlight.**

Right: **A substantial timber pergola encloses a terrace with filtered shade and support for climbing plants. Wrought-iron furniture is fitted with soft blue cushions. Classic, circular, sprung metal chairs sit at the table.**

boldly and simply, in groups or rows of a single design, and the planting should ideally follow similar rules. Pots that are overflowing with a single colour pelargonium are classics for a balustrade or staircase, whereas on a terrace, a row of large pots might each support an orange tree or a huge ball of fragrant rosemary (*Rosmarinus*).

Depending on their source, clays can vary in shade from creamy white, common in France, to the deep reds of Tuscany. This will obviously make a considerable difference to the overall look, so it is very wise to consider your paving and walls before making a selection. Shapes include the straight, tapering camellia pots which are plain with a bold rim and the wide-rimmed lemon

Below: **The visual strength of this terrace lies in its utter simplicity. A row of matching terracotta pots, which are effectively planted with a single variety of pelargonium, lines one side. The furniture is unified by the choice of black wrought iron, while the pink granite tabletop reflects the soothing tone of the floor and columns.**

Bottom: **When the weather is warm and the sun is shining, it's impossible to stay indoors.**

pots, simple with two applied bands, or highly decorated with combinations of flower and fruit garlands, attended by cherubs and gods. Olive jars with narrow necks and bases make good architectural decoration or water features, but make planting difficult, as it becomes impossible to remove the rootball once the plant is established.

Glazed terracotta is a speciality of southern France, with mellow colours falling mainly into three groups: dark green, deep blue and mustard yellow. The tall Anduze vase, narrowing at the top to a low neck and at bottom to a plinth, is a classic. Try to find "antiqued" ones: the "aged" appearance adds to the effect. Other countries make glazed pots, but they tend to be of brighter colours.

Left: **Pale clay bricks set in a herringbone pattern pave a vaulted terrace. The stack of square terracotta "pots" makes an inventive rainwater spout to one side of the arch.**

Below: **The stone archway frames the view and provides a compelling invitation to pass through the wisteria-clad pergola beyond.**

Right: **Magnificently crumbling doors frame the entrance to the terrace beyond. These hand-made, Italian terracotta "lemon pots" are true Mediterranean classics. Although each contains a different species, the look is controlled by consistently using pots with the same shape throughout the courtyard.**

To complete the essence of fine Mediterranean living, why not also include a lemon tree to garnish thirst-quenching cocktails and an orange tree to embellish a healthy breakfast?

Flowering climbers adore hot, sun-kissed walls, and the choice of plants for these conditions is immense. However, it goes without saying that the iridescent bougainvillaeas are many people's first choice. Orange, bell-flowered campsis and the heavily perfumed white jasmines will also make an authentic contribution to a Mediterranean setting.

The character of plants in the Mediterranean garden is crucial to the authentic finish of the design. In their native environment they have to survive in poor soil, low rainfall and scorching sun, so their foliage and root systems adapt in order to cope. As a result, only a well-drained and sunny site will accommodate them. Textural grey and silver leaves are common, some furry and some spiky. Typical examples are *Santolina chamaecyparissus*, *Anaphalis triplinervis*, *Artemisia ludoviciana* and the prickly, thistle-like eryngiums. Immensely tall cardoons (*Cynara cardunculus*) produce huge, blue, thistle heads, which dry well for winter flower displays. Blue flowers look stunning among silver-leaved subjects, and none more so than the stately agapanthus.

Needle-like, water-retentive leaves, like those of the conifers, proliferate in the Mediterranean climate, and they also often give off pungent scents. Many herbs produce essential oils, resulting in foliage that is aromatic when crushed. Classic subjects include rosemary, sage, bay, marjoram and thyme. Fruiting figs (*Ficus*) and a grapevine (*Vitis*) to shade the timber pergola are real must-haves.

S.L

japanese

The setting is a hillside covered in deep green moss, with paths winding past contorted tree roots and rocks. Clumps of tall bamboo rustle in the breeze; the delicate foliage of maples turns brilliant shades of vermilion in autumn, imitated by golden carp in gurgling streams. The feeling is of being at one with nature, a part of the living environment.

Left: **A bronze heron, fishing among the lily pads, introduces an element of humour and sculptural form to a softly rolling backdrop of acers and bamboo.**

Above: **This pine has been clipped in the traditional style of "cloud topiary" in which the growth resembles floating clouds. It is visually anchored by boulders and a box ball.**

Below: **This hut is just large enough for a diminutive gardener or a woodland god.**

Japanese gardening is less about decorating the surface and more about what emerges from the earth. There is a sense of the energy of life forces, whereby rocks and tree roots are at least as important as leaves and flowers. The approach is a total reverence for the beauty and integrity of nature.

Although it is difficult to recreate this picture authentically outside Japan, it is possible to capture its essence. Simplicity, natural materials and integrity are the keys to success. Develop your own sense of organic form, using rocks, driftwood and planting. By all means, introduce a stone buddha or spirit house, but avoid the overuse of kitsch symbolism where possible.

Traditional Japanese temple gardens are situated in stunning, naturalistic settings of mossy hillsides covered in tall maples, their sinuous roots clinging to giant rocks. Leaves turn every shade of gold and crimson in autumn, while lakes and streams are filled with exotic golden carp which flash in the sunlight. This method of garden design is known as "borrowed landscape".

Within the temple, garden areas tend to be focused to highlight particular styles or forms. These include bamboo plantations, background spaces devoted to maples, moss gardens, clipped topiary hedges and cloud pruning. The cascading blooms of trained wisteria are a special feature in spring, a time when overflowing cherry blossom creates an excuse for festivities in Japan. This season is so longingly awaited that weather forecasts include blossom reports all around the country.

Temples tend to be rectilinear, arranged with each room looking out across a veranda to an individual style of courtyard. This "viewing platform" is used for meditation, often incorporated with the tea ceremony. The concept of composing a picture to view from the house translates effectively to the West, especially when gardening in a small space.

An unpromising courtyard, roof terrace or even a narrow balcony, can be transformed into a tranquil private space by incorporating some of the traditional elements. Enclose your area with combinations of dried bamboo screening and string-tied trellis to provide privacy and shelter. Plan carefully to make the best possible use of available space and concentrate on building up scenes of asymmetric balance using combinations of weight, height, form and texture, in both construction and planting.

Above: **A rocky outcrop is dramatized by this crashing cascade of water, descending to stillness in the pool below.**

Below: **A small, thatched retreat in a glade provides a contemplative veranda from which to enjoy the peace of this cool pool.**

Wood combines well with Japanese styling and is appropriate in the form of timber decking. An elevated seating area, leading from the house, can be designed with further changes of level to incorporate stepped planting and a small pool. Where space is available, an extended boardwalk could take a passage through the garden.

Plants with clean lines like bamboos introduce elegant form and delicate, rustling foliage; they exist in species of many differing heights and colours, including black stems and striped leaves. Blocks or borders of the black bamboo, *Phyllostachys nigra*, make a stylish living screen in milder areas. Ornamental grasses and sedges can also be incorporated, as can the prehistoric horsetail, *Equisetum trachyodon*. In shady, moist corners, simple moss and fern areas can be cultivated.

Above right: **The tactile quality of these hand-sculpted boulders enhances their dramatic appearance. Here, they nestle among green sedges at the water's edge.**

Below right: **Rough timber planks form a sympathetic bridge across a shady pond; the clump of exotic plants and the bamboo water spout suggest a sort of watery oasis in the centre.**

Opposite (top left): **A sculpture of carefully balanced layers of flat stone subtly mimics the striated seedheads of quaking grass (*Briza*) that surround it.**

Opposite (top centre): **An impish Buddha sits smugly, wreathed in ferns.**

Opposite (centre left): **The spirit house is an important feature of Oriental garden design.**

Opposite (centre right): **The sight and sound of water surging through fern-covered rocks epitomizes the Japanese love of nature.**

Opposite (top right): **This handsomely carved spirit house makes a significant focal point between the garden and the woods.**

Opposite (bottom): **This brightly painted bridge makes a strong connecting statement between two parts of the garden. Specially designed gold finials emphasize the curve and movement.**

Evergreen, spring-flowering camellias and Japanese maple (*Acer palmatum*) for texture and stunning autumn colour can be sited individually or in groups. You can make your own specimen cloud topiary from box (*Buxus*) or conifers, inspired by the project on page 236–239. Stoneware is a traditional medium for containers, which can be sited in strategic spots. They are equally well suited to strongly textured palms and pines, or to clumps of ornamental grasses.

A sense of tranquillity and areas for contemplation are important elements in the Japanese garden. Water, the essence of all life, should always be present, and will help to create this ambience. In its simplest form, a stone bowl filled with water is calming, inviting birds to come and drink. In Japan, a spring would fill it via a bamboo pipe, and a bamboo ladle would be present to allow passers-by to take refreshment. This idea can be easily adapted into an attractive feature with the help of a small pump.

Moving water gives a sense of freshness and vitality. The effect of a stream washing over river pebbles would be a lovely idea, combining glinting reflections with the sound of bubbling water. A simple version would be fairly easy to construct using a shallow liner set beside a gravel path or decking. This could have water bubbling up through rocks that are piled up to just above water level at one end. The result is the soothing movement of water, without the need for a complex recirculating system.

In traditional Japanese gardens, paving is often made from combinations of pebbles and river stones arranged in geometric patterns, but, because of the natural irregularities of the material, the results have an informal quality. According to the source, colours vary from almost white, through pinks and greys, to almost black; the effect of rain extends these to deeper tones with a gleaming appearance.

The use of stones and pebbles is gaining interest in the West for both modern designs and less controlled rustic situations. Their rounded, irregular shape makes them ideal for circular designs and infill between planting areas. Although more expensive, whole pebbles are more pleasing in shape and texture than gravel; sizes range from 1–10cm (½–4in) in diameter, the smaller grades being most suitable for larger areas.

Rocks and stones have a special importance in Japan, with vast fortunes changing hands for prize specimens. The famous stone gardens, which some people consider to be cold and stark, are just one aspect of Zen Buddhist philosophy, but you can draw inspiration from them to create your own version. Choose some special stones of varying size, colour and character. Arrange them asymmetrically in one or two areas; uneven numbers of, say, three or five are best, and cover the rest of the chosen site with a layer of finer pebbles. These are then raked into variations of parallel lines and snaking spirals centralized on the main rocks. Clumps of green moss may be arranged around the specimens to provide a softening cushion, but to be completely authentic, no further planting should be included.

Opposite (top): **This Zen-inspired mask makes a striking statement surrounded by tall miscanthus.**

Left: **Adapted from a temple stone garden, this calm courtyard makes interesting use of sawn tree trunks to make paths through the gravel. Three handsome rocks stand sentinel over a tiny, bridged pool at one path's end, while the other leads to a sheltered viewing house.**

Below: **Bamboo wind chimes are attractive and create soothingly quiet sounds.**

seashore

Expanses of beach meeting crashing surf; sturdy little wooden huts painted ice-cream colours, all amid sand dunes and windswept grasses – this is untamed landscape, wild and free, beloved of artists and naturalists. If you have a yearning to break away, create the look in your garden and breathe in the fresh sea air.

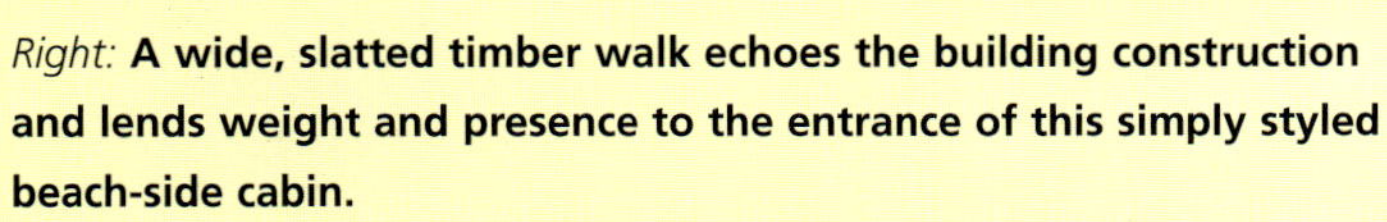

Right: **A wide, slatted timber walk echoes the building construction and lends weight and presence to the entrance of this simply styled beach-side cabin.**

Left: **Found objects can make excellent informal, and very often impromtu, sculptures. This still-life of rowing oars and a garland strung with pebbles sets an evocative scene against the timber-planked wall.**

Right: **Brilliantly coloured poppies make dancing shapes inside a circle of pebbles in this coastal garden.**

Below: **Pillars of stone-capped driftwood stand like maritime stalagmites among drifts of orange *Eschscholzia californica* and sea kale (*Crambe maritima*).**

The seashore recalls fun-filled outings and the exhilaration of bracing sea breezes, so why not make your garden a constant reminder of these sunny days by introducing elements of the seashore? When walking on the beach, especially in wild, exposed places, you can find exciting flotsam and jetsam washed ashore. Ropes, fishing nets, ships' timbers, redundant lobster pots and giant cable reels are all possibilities. These man-made objects can all be given a new lease of life, recycled in the seaside garden.

However, we must take account of our ecological climate when collecting objects from the seashore. Look, examine and take inspiration, but remember that shells, pebbles and rocks are part of a carefully balanced natural landscape, and we cannot just help ourselves. In fact, in many countries, collecting from the beach and the sea is illegal, even in tiny quantities, so please contact licensed suppliers, where you can source all the hard landscape materials you require.

Right: **Strongly textured agaves and eryngiums are softened by the delicate swathes of mauve-blue perovskias.**

Below: **This wide, flat beach-scape has been formalized by naturalistic parterres which are bordered with stones and flints. It is important to point out that cultivation in such a place is only possible with the incorporation of much organic matter. Sparkling, orange poppies provide just the right amount of colour to accent the pale, rounded hummocks of helichrysum and santolina and the yellow-painted window and door frames of the house.**

The seashore is constantly changing due to the actions of the wind and the tide, so the seaside garden should reflect this by sweeping informally in curved shapes. Straight lines and regularly shaped planting beds would look unnatural, so think instead in terms of drifts of planting. These can be set among shingle consisting, at its simplest, of inexpensive chipped flint stone. A more beautiful, though more costly, alternative is entire pebbles graded in size from a few millimetres to large stones. These have an authentic, natural character with the added dimension of subtle variations in colour.

Planting choices should reflect the windswept shore. There is a range of grasses to choose from, varying from short tufts to tall swathes. Graceful, narrow stems range from pale grey, through green to gold and white, with the added winter interest of seedheads that rattle in the breeze. This is an exciting group that will enable you to discover a new vocabulary of planting design with colour, texture, form and sound.

Safety and durability are important considerations when building out of doors. Decking must be constructed from durable hardwoods or specially treated softwoods. In moist climates, decks can become slippery and are prone to deterioration; boards with a ridged surface can help with grip, and so will regular brushing. Supporting structural timbers should be set in concrete, and no wooden part should be in direct contact with the earth.

To maintain the nautical theme, link the house to the garden with ships' decking made from timber boards. A raised terrace will make a wonderful sitting area from which to view the garden. You might also like to string out a canvas awning from the wall in order to shade the decking. This will make the whole experience of eating outdoors in summer much more pleasant. Changes of level and perspective can be achieved with timber walkways connected by steps.

Top left: **Natural associations work well in wild situations, as this seaweed fretwork shows.**

Left: **Beach huts could become sheds in a private garden.**

Above: **An elevated timber boardwalk makes a practical pathway across changing levels and boggy areas. It provides long vistas along the shore without disturbing vegetation.**

Maintain the timber regularly with a suitable preservative. Steps should be covered with wire mesh or incorporate a gritty, non-slip surface material. Ropes knotted through timber piers make effective balustrades and handrails; if there are small children be sure to add fixed, low-level, horizontal handrails.

The colours of this seashore style – faded blues like old denim and the greens of sea thrift (*Armeria maritima*) and seaweed – are

bleached by sun and wind. Textiles are canvas, duck and net, in plain colours or nautical stripes. Furniture is easy style: choose stripy deckchairs, swing a hammock between old ships' masts and make a feature seat from a rowing boat upturned on the shingle.

A garden shed can be transformed to look like a beach hut by painting it in vertical stripes of blue and white. If there is space, double it up as a studio with a veranda to make a private place to which you can escape and dream of the sea.

Top right: **Coastal buildings have to endure battering, salt-laden winds and strong sunlight. Preserved natural timber is relatively maintenance-free and unobtrusive in the seascape.**

Right: **This lovely chair is constructed from carefully chosen timbers which retain the shape of the original tree forks. It looks very much a part of the sea-washed landscape.**

contemporary

In our increasingly complex lives there is a growing need to simplify and edit. The contemporary garden, pared down to pure form and texture, can create an environment that is both stimulating and calming, uncluttered by complex images. It is based on well-engineered materials, used concisely, and complemented by a focused palette of planting.

Left: **A theme of circles distinguishes this intimate patio water garden. Tall towers of round steel planting trays are echoed horizontally by floating timber "lily pads", encased by metal bands.**

Left: **Changing levels have been utilized cleverly to provide a raised swimming pool and stepped planting beds, both formed from concrete. Steps tiled in terracotta are echoed in a perimeter shelf around the dining area.**

Below: **Bold steel tubes emerge from a pool, supported visually by the massive *Dracaena draco* and complemented by blue, concrete rectangles and square trellises beyond.**

Gardens are most successful when they reflect their surrounding architecture, so that house and garden complement each other. Contemporary gardens will therefore be most suited to buildings designed in the modernist period (1910–1940) or in the late 20th century. That said, any building of restrained formality might equally support such an approach.

The style is minimalist with an emphasis on simple forms, skilfully executed from quality materials. Advances in building technology have resulted in the emergence of many exciting new materials and special treatments to more familiar ones.

Steel, which can be polished and bright, stainless or rusted, may be used in sheet form, mesh and rod. It has a

multitude of structural and decorative functions, ranging from stairs and railings, arches and pergolas, to furniture and containers. Molten zinc is used to rust-proof steel, but in sheet form it can be made into containers or used to finish surfaces.

Concrete may be moulded into exciting shapes and finished with textured aggregates; it may be used for ground surfaces, walls and containers. Granite can be polished or hammered for use in walls and paving. Glass, mirror and acrylic plastic can all be used for screening or sculpture.

In today's gardens, much reference is made to the Japanese garden philosophy, so complementary natural elements such as stones and cobbles, timber and bamboo may be incorporated.

Left: **Versatile modern materials enable the creation of complex designs. Nylon canopies stretched between aluminium poles are both strong and visually light.**

Above: **Perspex (Plexiglas) is available in an enormous range of colours. It can be cut to any shape, is translucent and will not shatter.**

Right: **This highly charged water garden is constructed from *in situ* concrete with tiled borders.**

Top: **Simplicity of design, the effect of light and shadow and the versatility of concrete could not be better illustrated.**

Centre: **Steel wirework columns contrast with the yellow grid walkway above the pool.**

Bottom: **Horizontal limestone steps contrast with the strong vertical planting.**

Water is a crucial element in garden design, giving light, reflection, sound and movement. Combined with the imaginative use of construction materials in a contemporary design, water may be used to new and dramatic effect. Our contemporary water feature on page 246–247 demonstrates an innovative idea that you can easily recreate.

The balance of plants to hard landscaping means that their role is as much sculptural as horticultural. It is important to select plant material primarily with a view to its year-round architectural and aesthetic value, then be creative with form, making blocks and sweeps with single varieties. Select larger specimens, perhaps in pots, to make special features.

Plants with a strong vertical emphasis make good structural statements. There is a wide variety of bamboos available, ranging in height from 30cm–3m (1–10ft), with stems in colours from yellow and green to black, and with both variegated and plain leaves. Tall-growing varieties are excellent foils against high walls and make effective screening; shorter-growing species work well as an edging for paths. Tall grasses look terrific in large swathes, especially where there is some air movement to show off their sweeping habit. For infill areas, plant clumps of low-growing species with grey, hair-fine foliage. In winter, the grasses show off their shining, textural seedheads.

Opposite (right): **The terrace of a 19th-century building has been given a modern treatment.**

Below: **A cascade of water is disgorged from the massive, rust-painted screen dominating this small canal. The weight and form of the screen balances the presence of the nearby tree.**

Stately phormiums make tall clumps of narrow foliage in colours ranging from green to red-black, often with striped variegation; stunning, burnt-black seedheads stand on tall zigzag spikes in winter. Yuccas produce rosettes of narrow green leaves and a spike of huge cream flowers in late summer.

Succulent sempervivums have great sculptural value and are incredibly easy to maintain, needing virtually no soil and little water. They are best planted informally in gravel areas or in containers, where their low rosettes make an interesting contrast in scale.

The minimalist garden can be treated as a gallery space in which to display a piece of sculpture, or to experiment with exciting new designs of furniture and containers. The purist layout means that any object placed in it will be shown to full advantage, so take time to source pieces that are absolutely right.

It is refreshing to find designers who think especially of the garden when executing new ideas; specialist garden and decoration shows are a very good place to find them. It is now possible to commission a mirror-glass pyramid functioning as an accurately calculated sundial, around which you could base an entire courtyard design. Functional items are also taking on new forms: a steel and stone barbecue, so beautiful that it is almost a crime to cook on it, or a terrace heater shaped like a folding parasol.

Furniture made from aluminium and nylon, recliners formed from laminated steamed oak, and diminutive, acrylic plastic chairs all vie for attention. These are refreshing new concepts, often developed as lightweight, folding pieces suited to modern living and small spaces.

Opposite (bottom left): **A vertical, clear plastic tube allows an innovative view of bubbling water in this stylish feature.**

Centre: **A bold pink, concrete screen wall, through which a cascade of water descends, dominates this stylish pool. Horizontal elements of the house design are repeated through the doorway lintel, the water chute and the diving board.**

Below: **A courtyard is brought alive by a suggested water feature formed from transparent glass bricks and a "cascade" of mirror mosaic. Light is reflected into the area by the pale yellow walls and sand-coloured gravel. The foliage plants stand out strongly against the walls.**

Planted containers can be used as design features in their own right; you can reflect the pared-down look that is so popular among contemporary garden designers with tall and narrow shapes balanced with low, sculptural planting. Zinc, whether shining or patinated, and sheet-formed lead are the latest materials to find favour among garden designers. Made into simple rectangles, circles and tapering cones, they are both handsome and functional. Try making the container project on page 210–213; this enhances a simple timber planter by the application of a decorative lead grid. Concrete in innovative finishes and textures is also becoming increasingly sought after. Terracotta pots have always had a place in the garden; but it is best to choose oversized pots with any decoration limited to a simple rim.

the materials

Enormous amounts of time and energy are given to the selection of plants for the garden and this is understandable, as they are fundamental to its ambience and emotional appeal. However, without a similarly sympathetic approach to the choice of hard landscaping materials and a comprehension of their practical and visual roles, a garden design can so easily fail.

These materials provide the permanent elements of form, texture and colour in the garden and are thus responsible for its bones, the structure and integrity of the design.

There is a huge and wonderful wealth of materials from which to choose, and they are not just façade, but play a crucial role in defining the appearance and character of the garden. Through an understanding of their qualities, we can create backdrops that empathise, not fight with our planting choice and build structures that inject dynamism and vitality to our garden design.

We explore the different materials currently available for use in outdoor construction, covering the natural, composite and exciting new technology synthetics. You are guided through their individual qualities, examining the uses for which each material is most appropriate. Account is taken of relative structural and performance considerations, cost and availability, giving you all the means to arrive at your ultimate specification.

Above: **The light-capturing quality of stainless steel suits it perfectly to sculptural water features. The rippled flow of moisture over this smooth surface agreeably "muddles" the reflected images in the garden, while at night the backlit "moon" glows mysteriously.**

Left: **Glass combines wonderfully with water in all manner of special features. Parts of this unique design give the illusion that the water is moving upwards.**

Opposite: **The fine horizontal slats of this simple wooden sculpture contrast well with the bold, vertical garden fence posts beyond.**

stone

Natural stone possesses qualities that are both pleasing to the eye and gratifying to the soul.

It is always at one with the landscape, conveying a sense of place, timelessness and integrity. It is a sobering thought that much of the stone we now quarry was created thousands of millions of years ago. Its strength and huge variety of colour and texture make it one of the most seductive and enduring materials to use in the garden.

Left: **Smooth, pale limestone provides a clean, understated structure for this elegant formal garden. Its strong lines are reinforced by the rectangular forms of dark topiary and lawn.**

surfaces

Real stone paving adds character and gravitas to gardens of every style. The selection of material, the way it is cut and finished, and the laying pattern will all influence the final look, which can be traditional, rustic or contemporary.

Right: **A sense of movement is created by this snaking limestone path, emphasized by the dark granite slips infilling the spaces between the lines.**

Opposite: **Terrazzo can be moulded into curving shapes. Here, a strip of pebbles emphasizes the form of the polished areas.**

Below: **Massive spheres of natural stone contrast with cool, smooth paving.**

Stone mellows beautifully with age, and its wide range of texture, colour and finish makes it possible to choose stone to suit any scheme. When planning a large paved area, it is always most effective when the material blends with, or provides an intelligent contrast to, the existing architecture of the property, so try samples *in situ* before you decide. Both the colour and texture of stone may be affected by rain, so run a hose over the sample to ensure that it will look satisfactory in both dry and wet conditions.

"York stone" is a description now often applied to all sandstone paviors, though true York stone is quarried only in one region of northern England. Used as paving, it is strongly associated with the Georgian period in Britain, and the fact that so much survives in good condition testifies to its durability. The cost of new York stone is prohibitive, but reclamation dealers can usually supply old slabs, mainly from industrial sources, at a more accessible price. Reclaimed stone from such sources is sometimes suffused with machine oil, so check it out before accepting delivery. Riven sandstone slabs, which reveal the rock's laminated structure, are often used for traditional designs, while smooth-sawn paviours look clean and contemporary. Unlike manufactured paving, the thickness of natural slabs varies, so allow for this when laying to ensure a level surface.

Limestone is usually supplied as sawn slabs, producing constructions of an elegant, restrained appearance. The pale colours of this stone combine well with modern materials such as stainless steel and zinc, and this makes it an attractive proposition for new gardens. However, it is more absorbent and prone to erosion and acid damage than sandstone. Some varieties are considered to be harder and less porous than others, but all limestone has a tendency to stain. This makes it vulnerable to marking by spilt drinks and contact with the feet of metal furniture or other objects that may rust. In brief, it is a stone for grown-ups with controlled lifestyles.

Slate's laminated structure enables it to be split into plates, hence its traditional use as roofing tiles. It has great lateral strength, making it ideal for surfaces such as steps and paving. Slate paviours can be supplied riven, giving them an uneven, fragmented surface with a rustic character suited to naturalistic gardens. When the stone is smooth-sawn and buffed to a matt finish, it takes on a more disciplined appearance that works well over large areas and is appropriate for modern designs.

Granite is a sensible choice for paving because of its density and durability. Large slabs are costly and extremely heavy, but small, rectangular blocks, called setts, are conveniently sized for making curves and detailed inset designs. When finished with a hammered, slip-resistant surface, granite setts are a sensible choice for slight gradients and steps. Granite can have an overly severe appearance in a domestic situation, but to help integrate the setts with the garden you can fill the spaces with a sand and soil mixture and sow grass seed instead of grouting with cement.

Unlike these natural types of stone, terrazzo is a manufactured product that consists of marble chippings set in concrete and polished to a beautiful smoothness. It makes a highly sophisticated ground covering.

Generally thinner than paving slabs, facings are used to cover vertical surfaces such as walls and risers for steps. They are also appropriate for cladding the sides of raised formal pools and for all types of copings. While they do not play a structural role, they are used to give the appearance of solid stone to the finished structure.

Granite is a prestigious material that is frequently used for decorative facings. It is normally given a highly polished finish, revealing its dramatically fiery structure. However, this tends to give it a rather monumental appearance, so in domestic situations it is better restricted to small elements of detailing.

Polished slate also provides a gleaming, hard appearance, but at a lower cost and of more subtle tone. Smooth-sawn facings have an understated matt finish, well suited to urban courtyards and terraces. Slate offers dark and subtle shades that contrast starkly with the bright, crisply optimistic creamy shades of sandstone and limestone.

The highly polished finish usually given to marble leads to the assumption that it is durable, but it is formed from absorbent limestone and can be very unstable outdoors. It is prone to weathering and easily stained by contact with acids and rust. It is therefore advisable to restrict its use to protected situations or gardens in temperate climates, and it is perhaps best used for small areas of detailing, such as a contrasting border to a path, a surround for a formal fountain or a wall decoration. Pieces of various sizes, suitable for creating neutral-toned mosaics, are sold for just this purpose and look marvellous as inset relief, teamed with a floor of pale limestone or as a contrast to dark slate paving.

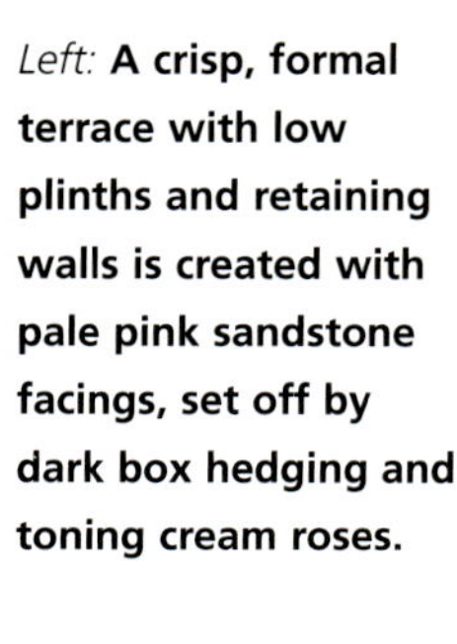

Left: **A crisp, formal terrace with low plinths and retaining walls is created with pale pink sandstone facings, set off by dark box hedging and toning cream roses.**

Right: **This formal pool is deliberately shallow to show off the unusual rectangular slabs of sawn slate used to construct both the liner and the surround. The water enhances the subtle colours of the stone, while loosely informal planting, framed by a screen wall of the same material, makes a delicate foil to the clean, architectural lines of the design.**

construction

Hard landscaping in stone provides the bones of the garden by establishing the lines of a formal composition to support the planting. It introduces focus and contrast by creating three-dimensional elements and structural features.

Above: **The wide, shallow limestone steps set the mood and scale of this formal, uncluttered terrace; the large size of the paving adds to the effect.**

Right: **A formal sweep of well-proportioned stone steps adds grandeur and pace to this large garden.**

Solid stone construction is expensive but gives the garden a wonderful feeling of solidity and presence. It is at its most effective when used in bold sweeps in a wide terrace, a dramatic wall or screen, or a gliding procession of steps.

The textural qualities of natural stone are demonstrated most effectively when combinations of rough-hewn blocks are used, perhaps to construct a decorative wall, such as the beautifully detailed screen shown opposite. The blocks of warm-toned sandstone lock together like the pieces of a jigsaw, without mortar or cement, presenting a very modern version of a dry stone wall. By contrast, a more rustic approach can be achieved with rough-hewn slabs being used to build structures such as retaining walls for plant borders or pools.

The finished look of stone facings is much more smooth and controlled than stone blocks or slabs, befitting a contemporary garden design. Facings are a more economical choice, although the cost of the basic structural work, which may be of concrete blockwork or poured cement, must also be taken into account. Stone facings are very effective so long as they are well detailed and carefully executed; the construction of such hard landscaping is costly, and almost always best left to the professional stonemason.

Opposite: **Fine materials and carefully thought-out detailing characterize this elegant screen wall. Constructed from vertical columns of dressed sandstone slips linked by smooth-sawn slabs, its pale, warm colours contrast delicately with the planting of fresh green grasses and deep purple iris.**

Terraces and steps extend the garden visually and provide interesting three-dimensional contrasts that are especially useful in town courtyards. Scale is very important when designing a garden, and steps are perhaps one of the most challenging features to get right. They can add immeasurably to the "presence" of the garden, imbuing even a smallish space with a feeling of dignity. They should be as wide as possible, in keeping with surrounding features, and must feel safe and inviting to walk on. A steep flight of shallow steps would be a challenge to climb and could seem threatening to descend. So follow the basic rule: the greater the difference in height between the upper and lower levels, the longer and more gradual the flight of steps should be. Design the steps so

Above: **Sawn slabs of dark slate have been built up at different levels to create this formal pool, over which a very shallow spill of water falls. The smooth buffed finish enhances light reflection, and the colour of the stone deepens attractively when wet.**

that each tread can be reached comfortably in a single stride, and allow a generously sized landing at the top and bottom.

When there are changes of level in the garden, structural retaining walls are required to contain the resulting terraces. Because of the weight and instability of soil, these need to be stoutly constructed on generous foundations, and provision must be made for rainwater to drain away freely. Retaining walls should be integrated into the design and may be multi-functional: if they can be built at a suitable height, they can double up as informal seating or be transformed into spaces for entertaining, like the innovative bar shown in the picture below, which effectively increases the use of the courtyard without compromising its scale.

Stone water features, such as pools and fountains, add to the garden ambience, introducing sound, movement, light and energy. Crisply cut slate lends itself to creating understated structures that allow water to spill quietly over its smoothly finished surface, while its neutral tones are equally suited to restrained paving, steps and copings.

Granite's robust character makes it an excellent choice for steps and retaining walls, though its high cost is likely to render large-scale use prohibitively expensive. Where a really dramatic presence is required, its distinctive colour and texture can be introduced as a single bold statement in the form of a substantial slab. Made into a striking bench, granite would make a bold contemporary feature.

Below: **Changes of level create visual interest as well as diversifying the usable space in a garden. Here, a low retaining wall faced with vertical slabs of slate permits an attractive backdrop of high-level planting. A curved bar of solid stone has been added to create an innovative entertaining area, paved with matching square paviours.**

sculptural effect

The textural qualities of stone can be exploited in numerous ways. It can be hewn into massive rocks or split into piercing spikes, carved into sensuously curving abstract forms or smoothed into spheres and obelisks.

Above: **A curved aperture transforms a simple limestone block into a dramatic sculptural seat.**

Right: **A revolving sandstone sphere makes a bold centrepiece for this formal pool.**

Opposite: **Slim slate pillars make a striking vertical statement in this garden, contrasting well with the massive boulders beyond.**

Limestone and sandstone, being smooth and easy to carve, are both popular for ornamental use. Figurative and abstract sculptural forms are normally placed as single statements, to provide a sensual contrast among plants. Geometric shapes, such as obelisks and pyramids, can play a more architectural role when placed formally to define an opening or focus a sightline.

A group of spheres of differing sizes can be very effectively arranged to make a Zen-inspired statement, while massive hunks of hewn slate and granite suggest powerful earth forces in an oriental garden. This works best when stones are placed in groups of uneven number, balancing differently sized pieces together. On a bed of raked gravel, the overall look is cool and severe, but it can be softened by adding clumps of turf or moss and small specimen conifers.

Interesting granite water features can be bought ready-made. Water is forced up through holes drilled in spheres and "millstones" to create a pleasing bubbling effect. This kind of fountain is easily set up with a pump and reservoir to make a beguiling feature.

Slate breaks naturally into craggy forms with immense character. It makes excellent dynamic statements but is perhaps most frequently associated with water in naturalistic cascades. To be convincing, these must be integrated carefully into the landscape on a naturally sloping site, and need a powerful pump to push the water back up. The large stones are extremely heavy and need expert handling.

aggregates

Small particles of any type of rock are collectively known as aggregate. Aggregates may be composed of sharp chips, or they may be stones that have been weather-washed or artificially tumbled to produce a smooth surface.

Right: **This informal curving pathway demonstrates how loose-laid slate fragments can be used to fill awkward or unusual shapes: the snaking mound of fresh green planting shows well in relief.**

Below: **Pebbles and cobbles of all sizes make an excellent ground cover beside beach-style water features.**

Inexpensive and easy to handle, aggregates are mainly used to cover large areas such as driveways. They are also very useful in small courtyards, where restricted access would make paving hard to install, and make excellent paths in country gardens, where architectural formality can look out of place.

For large areas, smooth shingle and river gravel are economical solutions. Though the yellow-brown tones of gravel are not easy to incorporate into a garden design, it is cheap and widely available. Beach pebbles are more attractive, with lovely colours ranging through soft pinks, greys and mauves. They blend into most landscapes, and are essential for Japanese and seashore themes. Grades of 10–15mm (½–⅝in) are about the maximum for walking on comfortably, while large cobbles and boulders make terrific landscaping features.

All loose materials move about and need regular raking to maintain an even surface. They also provide an ideal nursery bed for weeds, so spread a layer of fine gravel and cement, compacting firmly before covering with a thick layer of aggregate. Water thoroughly to bind the materials. A weed-suppressing membrane can be used instead, but the stones tend to slide on it, making walking insecure. It is, however, essential if you are making a dry gravel garden, in which case holes can be cut for planting.

A bed of contrasting coloured chippings in geometric patterns makes an interesting highlight in a courtyard. This is a purely

decorative, non-traffic feature that is the modern equivalent of formal bedding. Granite, limestone and slate offer subtle tones; white and black marble can be used to create a highly stylized effect. Polished river pebbles lend themselves to detailed mosaic in paved areas. They can be sourced in neutral colours such as black, grey and white to create very sophisticated designs. These are able to take foot traffic, so they should be set into a wet concrete screed.

Crushed slate, a by-product of quarrying, is useful for surfacing paths and makes a decorative mulch for beds and containers, where its soft heather tones suit most plants. It is perfect for Japanese-style "dry" gardens, where its subtle colouring and low surface energy can be successfully highlighted with dynamic, asymmetric groups of bold hewn rocks. A "dry river bed", a meandering ribbon of slate flakes arranged like naturally flowing water, makes an elegant alternative to a real stream. A sloping site is best, with the illusion emphasized by groups of larger rocks placed at intervals. These "streams" look especially attractive after rain, when the wet slate comes to life and takes on a lovely gleam.

Above: **Fine gravel, or pea shingle, makes an inexpensive and neutral ground cover for large areas. Here it plays the role of "white space", against which a formal planting scheme is clearly revealed.**

wood

The relationship of timber with garden construction is by far the most natural, as wooden structures have an innate affinity with plants. Wood is a warm, lively material, pleasing to the touch and the eye, and offers a wide variety of natural colour, tone and texture. It is easy to work with, and equally suitable for bold, strong structures such as pergolas and finely detailed work such as furniture and trellis.

Left: **Blurring the boundary between dry land and wet space, imaginative timber viewing decks appear to float like lily pads on this excitingly luxuriant pool.**

decking

The dictates of fashion now impose on the gardening scene as much as on the catwalk. It may seem that a layer of decking is covering the planet, but decking does provide an ideal solution to some common garden problems.

The huge popularity of decking is understandable from the point of view of versatility and ease of construction, but it is important to use it only where it is aesthetically appropriate.

Where weight is a consideration, such as on a roof terrace, decking makes a lightweight surface, and when outdoor space is at a premium, it can be an ideal way to create a raised seating area. A cantilevered deck, supported by pillars and guarded by a rail, can create a sun terrace with steps to a garden below. At ground level, the resulting "roof" could provide shelter for a children's play area.

A sloping site is a great challenge, but where different levels are required, decking provides an economical solution. Boardwalks generate a naturalistic feeling that associates particularly well with water and wild planting. Shallow wooden steps connecting the levels will create a series of easily accessible terraced beds, secured by rustic retaining walls of posts or recycled railway sleepers (ties).

The main downside of decking is that wet wood makes a good home for algae and can become slippery. Regular cleaning with a stiff broom or a power washer will help, and surfaces may also be covered securely with wire mesh. Grooved planks do not really aid grip, and a smooth finish looks better. If softwood is to be used, it must be of top quality. Compare cross-sections of different samples, and choose wood with fine, close grain, indicating slow-grown trees from well-managed plantations.

Above: **A boardwalk gives access to this bold pontoon built over a naturalistic pond.**

Right: **A raised edging provides a smart finish for a boardwalk.**

Opposite: **Decking is an ideal solution for dealing with changes of level in small spaces.**

boundaries and screens

Fences and screens give definition to a garden, and if made from wood they form a backdrop to the design, like flats for a stage set. The style, colour and texture can be varied, though they should support rather than dominate.

Below: **This unusual louvre arrangement makes a semi-opaque screen, providing an effective backdrop for planting and giving privacy to the house, while admitting daylight through the angled slats.**

Enclosures may be needed to give privacy from neighbours, hide an unwanted view or, in the case of a roof terrace, provide shelter from cold winds and excessive sunshine. The cheapest option is the traditional fence of wooden panels, which are available, ready for erection, in various grades. The most basic panels consist of overlapping rough-sawn softwood slats. Painting or staining them in a deep, muted shade such as grey or lichen green – both of which make a good backdrop for planting – distinctly improves their rustic appearance and often unpleasant colour. More stylish, heavy-duty alternatives, from specialist suppliers, are of better-quality timber and design, sanded and pressure-treated with preservative. Options include a choice of slat format, top rail profile and post finials. Special features, such as keyhole openings and trellis sections, make them useful for partial screening and garden division.

Composite wooden materials come into their own for instant makeovers and fun effects, especially when carefully detailed. Marine ply is a versatile medium for unusual designs, and even chipboard can be used, provided it is adequately sealed with an appropriate varnish or outdoor-quality oil-based paint.

Heavy, square-cut timber posts can be used to make dramatic, sculptural screening to delineate separate areas in the garden, emphasize a pathway or define a change of level. For a rustic effect, whole tree trunks make an interesting alternative, casting ever-changing shadows across the garden throughout the year.

Opposite: **This elegant screen is constructed from bold sections of treated, exterior-quality softwood.**

Above: **Steps leading to a dynamic moon window screen make a compelling invitation. Yacht varnish, used to seal the chipboard (an unusual, though economical, choice for the garden) also reveals its texture.**

Left: **This dramatic painted screen wall is made from sections of marine ply with insets of fins and louvres.**

pergolas and arbours

A wooden pergola provides an overhead "ceiling" for an outdoor area, while an arbour creates a secluded, romantic alcove. Both will contribute to the garden's overall ambience and will add enormously to the pleasure of your garden.

Its ready availability and ease of working make timber an excellent material for garden structures. Its organic origin makes it an especially sympathetic choice when the primary purpose is the support of climbing plants.

A pergola of wooden slats on strong timber pillars can be constructed over an existing terrace to create an atmospheric seating area that is shaded from sun and screened from overlooking windows. Weaving a fabric canopy through the slats gives extra privacy, and the timbers will take fixings for suspended lighting for use in the evening. More conventionally, a pergola can be trained with flowering and fruiting vines to give shade, colour and perfume.

The pergola is a useful device for delineating areas of the garden. When used in conjunction with a screen wall, a strong feeling of enclosure can be achieved, creating a change of atmosphere between it and the space beyond.

A freestanding arbour can make a dramatic architectural statement in a large garden. Clothed in fragrant climbers, a large arbour makes a romantic summer dining area. On a smaller scale, a seating arbour makes a good feature for a courtyard: a wooden bench sheltered by a framework of trellis panels doubles as an effective plant support.

Left: **This wide, vine-covered pergola provides much welcome shade and seclusion for this city rooftop garden.**

Opposite: **This pergola of western red cedar connects the walkway with the dining platform. Stainless steel battens support a glass canopy.**

roof terraces

Wood can be used to great effect in the construction and dressing of roof terraces. Hardwoods and softwoods can be worked into traditional and contemporary designs to create unique rooftop spaces that fulfil a range of practical needs.

Above: **Solid timber screens pierced with panels of openwork trellis serve to separate a hot-weather shower from the terrace seating area beyond.**

All roof terraces need some shelter, but the view is often an important part of their appeal and should not be totally obscured. Latticed timberwork makes an ideal protective screen, as it is both lightweight and versatile in application.

Roof terraces are especially vulnerable to the forces of weather – besides wind, there may also be freezing temperatures, driving rain, hail and snow, and sun. A screen intended to give protection from wind should never be solid, as this pushes the air up and over the barrier, creating an unpleasant cold down-draught. It should filter the wind and allow it to pass through gently. This is just as important for plants as for your own comfort, and on a roof terrace the wind is always likely to be much stronger than at ground level. Wooden screening provides essential protection for plants and allows dense layers of atmospheric foliage to flourish, which in turn will create its own microclimate.

An arrangement of narrow wooden slats with small spaces between them provides an elegant and effective solution. The modern design shown here demonstrates this, giving privacy without obscuring the view, while disguising the unsightly buildings nearby. The horizontal lines create a clear, open effect that emphasizes the impression of space. During the day, the interplay of sunlight and shadow makes ever-changing kinetic patterns across the walls and floor, while equally interesting lighting effects are achieved at night. Using wider slats

and spaces would alter the balance of light and shade, while a diagonal or square trellis pattern would entirely change the style of the terrace. Having a busier appearance, such an arrangement would make the space feel smaller, and this could be desirable if the aim was to achieve a feeling of intimacy.

With any raised terrace, it is especially important to pay attention to sound construction methods and fixings, and to ensure that the materials used are totally suitable. If wood is being used to construct guard rails and fences, the timbers must be secure and strong, and they must be regularly checked and well maintained.

Below: **The bold use of timber slats screens a roof terrace from sunlight, wind and prying eyes; by night, low-voltage lighting produces a softly glowing backdrop.**

concrete

Concrete provides an attractive and fairly economical solution in many situations, but it is probably the most misunderstood material of all time. Its bad reputation is the result of poorly conceived public projects in the 1960s and 1970s, but many renowned designers have chosen concrete to create elegant buildings and sophisticated engineering projects, and it is now being used for imaginative interior and garden features.

Left: **Concrete can be moulded into blocks or poured *in situ*, enabling the construction of complex shapes and forms such as this elegantly understated, formal contemporary pool.**

walls and screens

The simplicity of concrete construction enables pure forms such as screens, walls and backdrops to be created readily on site. Colour, texture and special finishes can be included to achieve a wonderful variety of special effects.

Opposite: **This spectacular lighting feature is created quite simply on a textured concrete screen wall set into a polished floor of the same material.**

Below: **Hand-polished concrete is a sophisticated finish for both walls and floors. Here, a pebble mosaic panel provides a decorative focus.**

Freestanding walls form a solid boundary to the garden, providing privacy, security and a clean backdrop to the design, while retaining walls hold back soil in raised beds and terraces. Within the garden, screens are an immensely useful device for breaking up space and can be used in differing heights and proportions to create illusions of distance and perspective. They may be pierced to allow glimpses of a secret garden or a surprising feature, inviting entry to the space beyond. Screen walls may also act as frames for inlaid "pictures" formed from mosaics of ceramic tiles, glass or natural stones.

The smooth finish that can be created with concrete is one of its main advantages when working with contemporary exteriors. Its neutrality and simplicity provide a clean backdrop and can give a real sense of scale and presence. Dramatic effects can be set against it, most notably using lighting to enhance a special feature. Cascading water really comes to life when lit at night, becoming an evocative focal point, while a plain wall throws up the changing silhouettes of architectural planting and allows sculptural forms to be shown off distinctly.

There are two ways in which concrete can be used to make a wall. The simplest is to create the structure from pre-cast concrete blocks, set on a foundation of wet cement and fixed together with cement mortar. This method is suitable for retaining walls and freestanding screens. A finishing coat of cement render may be smoothed to give a clean finish, or scratched over with a brush or nails for a textured effect. Colour tint can be included in the render mix or the finished wall can be painted when dry.

A concrete wall may also be poured into place. In this case, the wet mixture is supplied to the site and pumped into a mould or framework known as shuttering. Tints or decorative aggregates can be added to the mix, or decorative effects can be achieved by making the shuttering from textured materials, such as rough-sawn timber planks, which leave an impression of their grain on the surface of the concrete. For a very smooth finish, plywood or sheet metal is used as shuttering. *In situ* concrete construction is an exacting science and it requires specialist skill to achieve a perfect result.

flooring

Poured concrete quickly creates all kinds of flooring, including paths, terraces and steps. If necessary, shapes and dimensions can be amended easily on site, without the need for extensive planning and pre-ordering of materials.

Below: **This smoothly curved concrete path "glides" elegantly, in contrast with the rough-hewn, low stone planter and the stone gabion boundary wall.**

A floor is the simplest do-it-yourself use for concrete. After preparing the area with a bed of compacted hardcore, you need to make a simple frame from plywood or softwood and pour in the wet mix. A small concrete mixer, which can be bought or hired, will ensure an even supply of material and save hours of work. Having poured the concrete into the frame, release any trapped air bubbles by tamping down with a timber batten, then smooth over with a wooden float, ensuring that there is a slight fall to the surface to allow rainwater to run off.

Concrete has a tendency to expand and contract with changing weather conditions, so it is advisable to fill a large area in sections, leaving a gap or "expansion joint" of around 3mm (1/8in) between them. A large expanse of plain concrete can look grim and industrial, but you

can make the finish more interesting by inscribing designs into the surface before the mixture has set. Use a stiff brush, rake or sharp stick to create a pattern of lines, squares and circles, or even bare feet along a path.

An interesting organic appearance can be achieved with material such as leaves and stems. Leave them to set in the mixture, allowing their imprint to be revealed after decomposition. For a durable textured finish, aggregates such as pebbles or chippings may be added to the mix and exposed by gently brushing or hosing the surface just before the concrete sets. Alternatively, creative effects can be achieved by scattering material such as glass beads, shells or metal washers over the still-moist surface.

Right: **Exciting effects can be achieved by setting objects into wet concrete. Here, old spanners have been combined with coloured pebbles to make an innovative, eye-catching path at minimum expense.**

pre-cast paving

Pre-cast concrete paving is available in an assortment of styles and types. It offers a range of design possibilities and the opportunity to create modern or traditional flooring at a fraction of the cost of natural stone paving.

Below left: **Concrete paviours formed in natural stone moulds, such as these made to resemble riven York slabs, are very convincing and much cheaper than the real thing.**

Below right: **Curving paths are easily made from loose materials. Here, concrete slabs are laid in gravel to accommodate the increased spacing on the longer side.**

Taking into account the high cost of natural stone, pre-cast concrete paviours are a tempting option, especially for large areas. Though in the past these had a poor reputation and appearance, production techniques have improved enormously and some sophisticated products are now being created.

The current speciality in pre-cast concrete paving is very convincing replicas. There is an ever-increasing choice of slabs moulded from pieces of natural stone to give realistic surface textures, and respectable replicas of York stone, granite, terracotta and slate are all on offer. The natural-looking colours and finishes are extremely convincing, especially when a sympathetic laying pattern is used. Where a simple, understated effect is desired, it is possible to obtain excellent, smooth slabs in tones varying from creamy white through taupe to deeper grey tones that work perfectly well with contemporary garden design schemes.

Concrete paviours will not weather down, so choose your colours carefully, preferably checking the effect when both wet and dry. Cheap products have only a surface coating of colour, which can easily chip, revealing the plain grey cement inside. To avoid this, choose from among the more expensive options, which use quality pigments that are consistent throughout the slab. If in doubt, ask to have a slab broken to check before purchasing.

It is best to select a colour and texture that blends with the surrounding architecture. Subtle tones such as pale buff "sandstone" or greyish "slate" will blend well into the background of most gardens, while warm "terracotta" would

work well on any sunny Mediterranean-style terrace. York stone replicas are effective in the context of traditional garden designs, while fake granite setts can be introduced into both modern and classical gardens.

A simple laying pattern always works best with pre-cast paving; busy designs can look confusing and tend to make areas look small and congested, while clean straight lines extend the eye to give a feeling of distance and space. Contemporary-style square tiles require a formal layout on a square or diagonal grid. However, extensive paved areas can benefit from detail strips or borders in a neutral contrasting colour, such as black or cream. Irregularly shaped slabs, in shades based on natural stone, tend to look best, and more natural, when set less formally in a staggered pattern.

Left: **Smooth and simple, these white concrete paviours are the perfect foil for the organically styled Japanese planting.**

Below: **Clean architectural lines determine this formal planting scheme. To add a sense of dynamism, the square concrete slabs are laid in a diagonal pattern, contrasting with the clipped cubes of topiary underplanting the trees.**

glass

Glass is a vibrant and life-enhancing material that can be glitteringly clear or mysteriously translucent, admitting light but retaining privacy. Its colours may be jewel bright or softly subtle, and its surface can be etched or screen-printed for a multitude of special effects. Created by fusing minerals and sand at fantastically high temperatures in a molten state, it can be produced in flat sheets or three-dimensional shapes by moulding or blowing.

Left: **Freestanding etched glass screens in this courtyard provide sympathetic separation from the space beyond, ensuring a visually clean backdrop for the graphic planting design.**

surfaces

Glass can make an unexpectedly exciting contribution to ground cover in modern garden design, with streams of luminous glass chippings flowing around the planting to give theatrical effects of colour, light and texture.

Right: **The fashion for mosaic planting, here using clipped box balls, calls for imaginative contrasting mulches, like these brilliant blue glass chippings.**

Below: **Fantasy and reality mix at garden design festivals: in this example, a chequerboard of glass squares floats between gloomy pondweed to create a startling water feature.**

Glass chippings have become very modish as a landscaping material and can be most effective in limited applications. This recycled aggregate is available in numerous colours and size grades. For practical purposes, it is best used over more manageable areas of the garden.

For dramatic effect, chippings make an excellent, stylized ground cover, working well as a colour contrast for contemporary evergreen mosaic planting. Small areas, such as around planted tubs, work well too; both applications benefit from the use of a water-permeable membrane to separate the glass from the soil. Although often suggested as a general decorative mulch, this use is not highly recommended for reasons of maintenance: it is next to impossible to remove fallen leaves, and soil has a tendency to work its way up amongst the pieces. Wherever chippings are used, it should be possible to run a hose through to clean them. Tumbled chippings do have their sharp edges removed, but caution should always be exercised when handling them.

Glass aggregate looks really good when underlit at night. Spread it thickly over sealed laminated glass lighting panels, which can be incorporated into a geometric layout of paving and mono planting. Chippings are also effective when combined with water features, especially when used with lighting.

Opposite: **A fantastical, organically designed garden demonstrates the textural use of recycled glass in place of paving and ground cover planting.**

walls and boundaries

The existence of strengthened glass now makes it possible to create entire transparent walls around the garden, thus creating an invisible safety barrier or wind screen on a high-level terrace without spoiling a spectacular view.

Below: **Clear plate-glass panels provide security and protection from wind without obstructing the view from this terrace.**

The use of glass outdoors is a glamorous and ambitious concept, and its value is now increasingly appreciated in modern apartment developments, where every bit of space is valuable and every view desirable. Glass boundaries are now almost obligatory for luxury urban roof terraces, especially when overlooking a river or spectacular architectural panorama. The benefits of glass are twofold: as well as giving access to views, it allows light in, making it useful for small or shaded spaces, where it creates an immediate feeling of space and light.

Glass is an excellent solution for high-level situations, where protection from wind is required, as the heavy transparent panels give total shelter without any consequent loss of vision. However, it should be borne in mind that an invisible wall could prove to be hazardous to people and animals entering the space. In this case, an abstract pattern or a relief of stems or leaves could be etched on to the glass surface, serving both as decoration and a subtle security alert. Totally opaque sandblasted sections can be incorporated where some privacy from neighbours is desirable.

Toughened glass makes an excellent safety barricade around a roof terrace, still allowing the scenery to be enjoyed in full. Courtyards often have raised levels incorporated, which are usually protected by a timber or steel balustrade rail. A clear glass wall that creates no visual sense of a barrier would be a much more desirable safety device.

Cost is an inevitable factor when working with toughened glass, and the cost and complication of installation is a significant factor when using the material outdoors. It is therefore likely to be most accessible, in budgetary terms, when used over relatively small areas, or where the value of its physical contribution far outweighs its price.

Glass blocks have long been used to build interior walls, and they provide an equally effective device for enclosures and divisions outdoors. The thickness of the blocks makes them very strong, which means they can form part or the entirety of a substantial solid wall. Clear transparent blocks transmit the most light, though rippled and frosted finishes provide an extra degree of privacy. Coloured versions, in pale blue and green, are available for specific applications, especially in a pool area, where they make an ideal shower or dressing screen. Their somewhat retro appearance will not suit every garden, however, so they should be used only in simple modernistic schemes. Ensure that the blocks are suitable for outdoor use before you buy them. It is also advisable to have them installed by a specialist.

Glass blocks make interesting punctuation in a solid concrete wall, admitting light and making a contribution as a design feature in their own right. Peephole windows will admit light and reduce a feeling of claustrophobia in a walled garden. Rectangular, round or ovoid in shape, they can be formed from fixed panes of transparent glass to break up a blank space while providing an interesting view beyond. Where this would be inappropriate, perhaps in close proximity to neighbours, the choice of sandblasted glass would retain privacy without compromising on light levels.

Above: **A glass brick wall offers shelter without losing light. The staggered edge gradually opens up the view.**

Above left: **The visual weight of this wall is relieved by panels of glass bricks.**

screens

Glass has huge creative potential in its molten state, and there is an increasing number of exciting modern artists who are responding to its fluidity and can be commissioned to devise spectacular effects for a contemporary garden.

Opposite: **An opening between panels of embossed glass gives a tempting glimpse of the garden beyond, while the fine tracery of the design provides a visual link with the flowering tree.**

A multi-coloured glass panel introduced into a plain screen wall can create a sensational effect, especially if it is positioned to take the best advantage of sunlight. The changing effects of light and colour on the surrounding space add a particularly vibrant dimension to both the architecture and the planting around the wall.

Freestanding screens are often used in garden design to break up space, and they have a strong sculptural and architectural potential. Translucent or opaque coloured glass has a dramatic impact when formed into panels focusing on combinations of colour and shape for its effect. The screens can be used singly as a feature in a courtyard or in banner-like groups to introduce a walkway, letting sunlight through to look like a version of a Mondrian painting.

Glass treated with special finishes or effects permits very sophisticated decorative elements. One of the most exciting new possibilities is screen-printing images directly on to the surface of the glass. The results can be subtle and abstract, perhaps using out-of-focus shots of leaves and landscape, or dramatically eye-catching, with a blown-up flower detail or a piece of sculpture. Such pieces work best as tall screens in a clear space, where sunlight can bring out the images to their best advantage.

Right: **This textured screen makes a delicate sculptural statement in a romantic garden.**

Far right: **Use of colour backdrops can sometimes turn quite ordinary glass panels into something quite extraordinary.**

mirror

Reflections play an important dynamic role in the garden, but they need not always be provided by water. Mirror creates delightful surprises in an outdoor setting and can transform a space of any size with magical images and illusion.

Below: **A creative and amusing use of mirror as *trompe l'oeil*: a plain house wall is totally transformed by unexpected reflections of the garden.**

Reflected images in a garden can cause surprise and shock, introduce additional light and the illusion of spaciousness, or create magical sculptural effects.

Tall, vertical panels of mirror glass work brilliantly in staggered groups, especially in an area planted with a single type of plant, such as tall, slender grasses that sway in the breeze, where the reflections will multiply the effect of the planting. Placed horizontally, mirrors can form an illusionary bridge reflecting the sky. When mirrors are placed to reflect each other, the combination of reflected light and repeated images suggests a limitless kaleidoscopic landscape and offers numerous possibilities of interpretation in both large and small gardens.

Where space is restricted, in an enclosed courtyard or a narrow passage, strategically placed mirrors can double the perceived space by reflecting the area opposite. It is possible to play tricks like glazing a false door in a boundary wall, thus suggesting a landscape beyond that is merely the planting in its reflection.

By reflecting light, a mirror can brighten a dingy and otherwise unusable part of the garden. When used in conjunction with a fountain, it could completely enliven a dark, formal courtyard, multiplying the glinting effects of moving water among a planting of cool green ferns.

Always use mirror glass that has been specifically manufactured for exterior use, as you will find that the reflective backing of an interior mirror will peel off very quickly with weathering. Mirror is very heavy, so particular attention needs to be paid to fixing; for safety, always screw the glass securely to a backing of marine ply, which can then be bolted to a sound wall. Alternatively, set the glass in concrete foundations in the ground.

Opposite: **Mirror can provoke a reaction of surprise or disbelief. A raised "boardwalk" of panels dissects staccato grass plantings with reflections of the sky.**

light

Combine the sparkle and reflectiveness of glass with electric light, and a magical night-time atmosphere can be achieved, creating brilliant effects and unexpected silhouettes against the backdrop of the dark, mysterious garden.

Above: **Up-lighters in the pond and against strategically placed rocks lead the eye to the coloured light boxes in the distant rocks.**

Right: **Projecting light on to this glass box filled with white sea pebbles makes a highly textural night-time decorative effect.**

Floor lighting is a useful security feature on a formal terrace but can also provide subtle light-wash effects. Conventional up-lighters set in sealed glass discs are quite commonplace, but with imagination, and a skilled installer, it is possible to extend the concept radically.

Large panels of laminated glass, underlit with low-voltage lamps, can turn a whole terrace into a huge, magical light source. By contrast, long narrow strips would create a dramatic light border around the edge. Set into the paving, such lighting fulfils both decorative and practical roles in a classically modern scheme, and could be further extended to provide glamorous illuminated steps and wall features.

For special effects, lightboxes can be incorporated into walls, to look like night windows, or set in the ground surrounded by planting. A huge screen of opaque glass could serve as a dramatic backdrop for a sculpture, showing it in silhouette at night, or could make a bold contemporary statement in its own right. Small clear glass boxes look effective when filled with shells or washed river pebbles, while coloured glass glows with kaleidoscopic effects.

Safety must always be the first consideration when working with electricity out of doors; have all fittings professionally installed and checked.

Opposite: **Modern technology begs the imagination to take advantage. In this luxurious town garden, glass boxes containing lighting strips are set into decking to create subtle illumination and a marvellously intimate ambience at night.**

metals

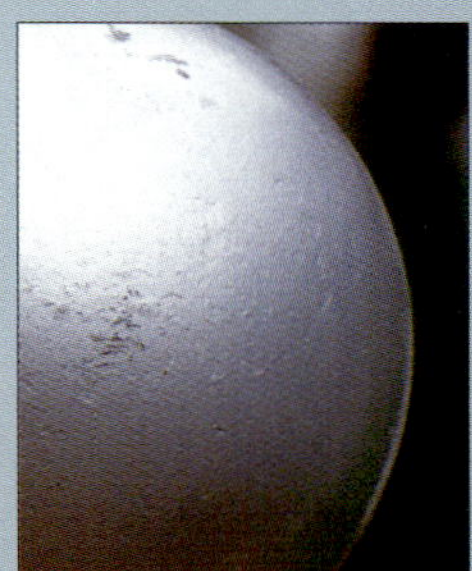

Metals are vibrant and elegant, with tremendous strength belied by light visual weight, making them among the most varied and versatile materials available. In flat sheet form, they are suitable for planters and surfaces, while metal rods and bars can be twisted into composite structures, such as gates and pergolas. Metals vary in strength, weight, texture and colour according to their mineral content, and this dictates what can be produced with them.

Left: **This lively garden is partitioned by huge, double-faced, steel mesh screens filled with cobbles. Amusing squares of deep blue plastic – their shape reflected in the bold timber seating cubes – relieve what could otherwise be a brutal effect.**

gates, railings and screens

Most gardens are enclosed by boundaries that form an integral part of the property's security arrangements. Gates and railings made from metal can provide a secure barrier without blocking the view, either into or out of the garden.

Below: **This boldly textured stainless steel gate contrasts effectively with the smooth surface and eccentric lines of the concrete boundary wall.**

Gates and railings are a traditional method of enclosing space and preventing entry. Metal railings are very strong, but in order to give them structural support, they are frequently incorporated with brickwork or stonework in the form of low walls, piers and gateposts.

Wrought iron, the original artist's metal, has been heated and hammered by blacksmiths for centuries into elaborate railings and gates. Its malleability, strength and visual lightness make it an obvious choice for intricately curving designs, often based on organic forms such as leaves and stems, which sit well among plants and trees in the garden environment.

Steel, a highly refined form of iron, has now largely taken its place. It is stronger and heavier, though more challenging to work and needing protection against rust. A material of great character, it is heated in a forge then twisted into shape, the various sections being welded together by hand. It can be made into staggeringly dramatic designs in both period and contemporary styles. This is highly skilled and demanding work, which is consequently very expensive to commission. However, simpler ready-made designs are widely available from specialist suppliers and are very well priced.

Stainless steel is playing an ever greater role in modern garden design. Television makeover programmes may seem to be largely responsible, but the trend is really a development from the increasing tendency to use this material for objects and fittings inside the house. It is, however, a very expensive material that needs specialist fabrication and installation.

Stainless steel is available in sheet form. It can be used flat or formed into undulating curves, and is especially appropriate for dramatic reflective screens and walls. The material would be visually overwhelming as an unrelieved mass, but the effect can be lightened by cutting out shapes and profiles by laser. These might be bold geometric forms, such as combinations of rectangular slots, or softer shapes – a slender

Above: **A steel louvre screen partially obscures one area of terrace from the other, while allowing some light to penetrate.**

Left: **Extensive, and unusual, use of copper cladding on this apartment development gives the buildings a warm, mature look that sits comfortably alongside timber decking and balcony screens.**

willow leaf, for example, would provide a link with the landscape, as well as being an excellent foil for what can otherwise seem a rather aggressive material. Perforated sheet stainless steel, die-cut with squares or circles in a range of grids and grilles, can now be obtained from specialist suppliers. This material has an industrial feel combined with an attractive visual lightness, which can be very effective in a modern garden design. It is excellent for making semi-transparent fences and screens, especially when used in conjunction with raised pathways or steps in a similar material.

Multi-stranded steel wire ropes are now almost obligatory on sleek, contemporary roof terraces. They combine incredible strength with low visual impact, making them an excellent device for use in safety screens and balustrades. For total security, the wires must be fixed under tension between posts, set at suitably short distances apart. Hardwood handrails provide solidity for the framework and have an appropriately nautical feel, especially in a river or coastal location.

Tensioned wires make excellent climbing plant supports that are strong enough to carry the weight of vegetation without compromising its appearance. Fix them horizontally at regular intervals on a wall or fence, allowing a small space behind for tendrils to take hold. Alternatively, make a freestanding screen with a framework of timber battens, between which the wires can be stretched in a similar fashion.

Opposite: **Freestanding screens make excellent punctuation marks in a design, creating textural contrasts and backdrops to planting.**

Above: **Courageous design and imaginative detailing can achieve impressive results in a fairly small space. Here, fabulous torches transform a contemporary garden into a theatre of light and energy at night; the shimmering steel enclosing walls increase the intensity of the effect.**

Left: **A curving screen of steel mesh successfully divides this airy terrace into two more intimate areas, while retaining the sense of wide-open space.**

pergolas and plant supports

The special qualities of metal come into their own when constructing three-dimensional features in the garden. Its combination of physical strength and visual lightness makes it the perfect material for plant-supporting structures.

Right: **Patinated steel angle sections provide an original structural support for a broad timber rail, creating a simple and effective contemporary pergola.**

Below: **Screen walls of steel reinforcing mesh provide support for plants on this large pergola.**

Arbours, pergolas, arches and gazebos must be strong enough to support heavy climbing plants and to withstand extreme winds. When built of timber, they are necessarily stout and solid, but structures made of steel can look relatively delicate without compromising their stability.

Traditional designs in curly "wrought iron" remain firm favourites for gardens in both town and country and can be bought ready-made or commissioned from an artist-blacksmith. These tend to look most comfortable with period houses, however; for a garden in modern style, check out garden shows and magazines for the fresh new formats that are now available.

Tall obelisks and cone-shaped plant trainers, in galvanized or rustic iron, make good punctuation marks, either as stand-alone features or to introduce a three-dimensional element in a planting bed.

Stainless steel structures suit a cutting-edge garden scheme, particularly if they are sensitively designed to reflect the style and details of the property. The metal can be given either a satin or a shiny bright finish, each with its own character. A sleek, sweeping pergola would look sensational over a dining terrace, while an archway or tunnel could frame a staircase. Visually light materials such as glass, Perspex (Plexiglas) and nylon might be incorporated as screens or canopies, while hardwood provides a contrastingly solid form of detailing for handrails and steps. Such structures are definitely in the luxury bracket, however.

Above: **The fantastical use of twisted wirework, exemplified in this adorable French-style confection, goes in and out of fashion, but the time and skill required to make such a piece means that such items are now rarities.**

Left: **This rusted steel arbour demonstrates an original use of ironwork. The contemporary feel, combined with the organic form reminiscent of a globe artichoke, is in wonderful contrast to the traditional walled kitchen garden in which it stands.**

surfaces

The practicality of industrial metals is now being taken advantage of in contemporary garden design. Brilliant stainless steel appears on terraces, while mesh grids make elegant pathways through groves of bamboo.

Opposite: **Gravel can be tiring to walk on, but an overlay of steel mesh provides an attractive, secure path.**

Below: **Intimacy is achieved in a formal pool with pink lighting glowing through both the shiny steel mesh walkway and the water.**

Below right: **Textured stainless steel sheet makes an unusual decorative cladding for this timber post.**

Sheet stainless steel is too costly, and perhaps too aggressive, to use for a whole floor area, and can become uncomfortably hot in sunlight. However, if its use is restricted to smaller areas, a slick element of brilliance can be introduced to a contemporary garden. A steel pathway cuts a real dash through a planting scheme, the textures of the metal and the foliage contrasting dramatically. A shiny steel detail would add a glamorous touch to a hardwood deck or dark slate paving. Depending upon the desired result, smooth reflective or satin finishes are available; for a more textured effect, try stainless steel sheet embossed with a raised pattern.

Galvanized steel mesh, which is traditionally found in industrial settings and on fire escapes, makes an excellent, non-slip tread for steps. Its free-draining quality renders it eminently suitable for raised walkways, and it can also be used to give an edgy feel and secure tread to gravel paths.

Stainless steel would make a luxury, hard-working tabletop for a bold timber base, though more accessibly priced zinc, the time-honoured surface of French bar counters, is seeing renewed popularity in this role. Its resistance to corrosion makes it practical for exterior use, and its original shine soon weathers to a matt finish that looks very comfortable outdoors.

Zinc's pliability makes it quite easy to handle in sheet form, a quality it has in common with copper, the luxury option. Copper has the added advantage of a colour unique among metals: naturally a warm golden brown, it starts out very bright but with exposure to moisture it quietly weathers to a glorious turquoise verdigris patina.

terracotta, ceramic and brick

Terracotta, literally "baked earth", is a sensual material that blends easily into the natural environment. Though mainly associated with pots, it is just one of number of different products made from clay, deep layers of which are deposited over large areas of the globe. Reflecting a wonderful range of tones and colours, clays are moulded and fired to produce a rich variety of building blocks, bricks and ceramic tiles that bring warmth and texture to the garden.

Left: **Handmade bricks have a unique quality and texture. This low retaining wall combines a mixture of colours, ranging from deep red to black, with a simple bond pattern to create a deliberately rustic effect.**

floors, steps and paths

Paving and groundwork in the garden have the same importance as parquet or tiled floors indoors. Clay tiles provide a practical surface and an uncluttered background against which furniture, decoration and planting can stand out.

Opposite: **Reminiscent of an Arabian palace, this path is made of richly coloured tiles in traditional patterns.**

Right: **Golden terracotta adds warmth to dark green planting.**

Below: **Dark bricks define the eccentric shape of this terrace.**

Tiling provides a convenient and attractive floor covering, with colours, textures and finishes to suit any design scheme. Tiles are perfect for terraces and small courtyards and particularly valuable for awkward situations such as narrow paths and steps. Paviours and floor tiles are available in a wide range of earth tones, from pale buff through to browns and blacks. The surface may be smooth or rough-textured, and this is a worthwhile consideration if the area is in danger of becoming slippery.

Floor tiles are usually plain, and simple layouts generally prove the most effective. However, details in a contrasting pattern, colour or tile size can make a good visual break in a large expanse. Decorative borders can frame a plain terrace or path, while panel insets create distinctive focal points.

Handmade terracotta tiles have a lovely texture, and their slightly uneven surfaces combine to make a very attractive floor that is rustic yet sophisticated. They come in a wide colour range, from very pale, which looks particularly effective when set off by a relief of deep-toned insets, to deeper shades. The latter are often found with a distinctive brindled effect that tends to look best laid alone. Machine-made tiles are a cheaper option. They are usually smoother, with less character, but their regular shape makes for easy laying. When selecting terracotta tiles, remember that many are low-fired and porous, making them unsuitable for exterior use, so check for frost resistance and

general suitability before ordering. They often need sealing to protect against water penetration and staining.

Simulated terracotta tiles, made from tinted cement, are economically priced and very hardwearing. Because of their regular size and shape, they are also convenient to lay. Vitrified clay quarry tiles may also be considered as a durable, less expensive, alternative to terracotta, though they lack its character and textural subtlety. Because they are non-porous, they are excellent for utility paving, and their red, brown and black colours give them a suitably low-key appearance. Fully vitrified brick paviours are much more handsome. They are very tough and can be obtained with a secure, non-slip finish.

Tiles must always be laid on a firm concrete base, and thick paving tiles should be set in wet cement. Bricks are fairly easy to lay on a well-prepared bed of hardcore, sand and cement. Most are made for walling and are therefore too crumbly for use on the ground, unless you are intending to achieve a vintage effect. Ask your supplier for a type suitable for your needs.

Brick flooring evokes period country gardens, though it can work well in an urban environment. Dark engineering bricks work brilliantly in contemporary gardens. Their small scale is especially suited to intimate courtyards, while brick paths make efficient linking or dividing devices among areas of planting. Some attractive patterns can be achieved, including basketweave – a busy design that tends to make spaces seem smaller – and herringbone, which is relaxing to the eye and has a gentle directional slant that works well for paths and larger terraces. Brick borders and patterns can be combined effectively with stone or cement paviours to add interest to a bland area.

Above: **Terracotta tiles laid like bright stepping stones among the creeping greenery make an attractive, informal garden pathway.**

Left: **Warm red brick steps lead irresistibly to a romantic timber clapboard house. Note the edging, which is correctly detailed with bricks set lengthways.**

Opposite: **Decorative tiles turn these steps into a linking feature between the house and pool.**

walls and constructions

It is the greatest desire of many people to have a garden enclosed by walls, and it is hard to deny that bricks – elegant, warm in colour and texture and sympathetic in scale – can be an extremely attractive medium from which to build them.

Below: **Texture is one of the most important elements in the hard landscaping of a courtyard or small garden. Sandstone paving reflects the tone and texture of the high brick wall in this courtyard setting, and the combination forms a blank canvas for the details of the courtyard, such as the furniture, containers and planting.**

Bricks are an extremely versatile building material with a comfortable domestic scale and character. They are made to a standard size and can be arranged in interlocking patterns to build vertical constructions of differing thicknesses.

The overall look of the finished work is controlled by the different laying patterns, known as bonds. English bond, the classic design for a garden wall, is created by alternating pairs of bricks laid side by side lengthwise (stretchers) with others set on end (headers). The result combines strength with an elegant pattern. There are many traditional bonds, and it is worth looking at built structures to see how much more distinguished some of the older, more complex patterns can be than the plain stretcher-style bond that is used today.

Freestanding walls make beautiful garden boundaries and may also be used as screens within a garden. They offer good support for climbing plants as they retain a lot of heat from the sun, encouraging the growth of more tender climbers and espaliered fruit trees.

It is always important to respect the surrounding architecture when selecting construction materials for garden use. Care should be taken when choosing bricks to ensure that they will be in keeping. Brick and terracotta seldom combine well with creamy stone houses, for example. If you are thinking of building walls near an old brick-built house, consider using secondhand bricks, which have more character than new ones, and can be obtained from specialist suppliers to match existing brickwork.

Bricks are an ideal medium for built features in the garden. The small size of the individual elements gives them enormous flexibility, making it possible to create curves and complex forms. Steps of varying height, width and depth are simple to achieve, and complex flights of angled or curving stairs can be built. A formal raised pond, a wall fountain or complex water features, including multi-level cascades, are all possible. Slate or stone copings and the careful choice of the surrounding floor details give a professional finish.

Small gardens benefit enormously from built-in features, which save space and keep the area looking uncluttered. Incorporating a brick-built barbecue and fitted bench seating in a patio design makes an excellent entertaining area, and is a particular boon in a tiny courtyard. Brick benches with removable timber lids can double as storage boxes for tools and garden supplies to save even more space.

Square brick piers make excellent supporting columns for a pergola or entrance gates. Though more difficult to construct, a circular brick pillar supporting a planted urn makes an extremely distinctive stand-alone feature.

Glazed ceramic tiles come into their own in the garden for special decorative effects. Their dazzling range of colours permits the creation of dramatic patterns that are especially relevant in gardens with tropical and Mediterranean themes. Tiles are eminently suitable for covering any surface, including walls, screens and tabletops, while single decorative panels provide

Above: **This curved freestanding wall creates a boundary between parts of the garden and provides warmth and shelter for the tender perennials in front of it.**

Right: **Brick is a very versatile material for all kinds of construction: rectangular shapes are straightforward, and it is also possible to create curving walls, such as this pool.**

interesting features to relieve plain rendered walls or screens. There is plenty of scope for creating exciting designs in dramatic combinations of colour, perhaps using broken tiles to "paint" a picture in mosaic.

Features such as fountains and benches built from basic blockwork can be transformed by facing them with coloured tiles. Curved objects such as formal raised pools present no problem with this treatment, and it is even possible to create fantastical sculptures decorated with small pieces of broken tile.

Coloured tiles look very effective combined with water and are frequently used to line fountains and swimming pools, for which they are an attractive, hardwearing and hygienic solution. Any size can be used, though mosaic tiles are popular for intricate designs. These tiny pre-cut shapes, which must be specified for outdoor use, are especially suited to creating patterns and covering curved surfaces. As colours tend to look brighter under water, you should be careful when choosing tiles for a large expanse like a pool, or the result can be unnaturally vivid.

Exterior construction work is a serious matter, and large brick structures, especially high walls, must be built with extreme care. Deep, solid foundations are needed, and sound bricklaying skills are required to achieve a smooth and elegant finish. Added to this, the cost of materials is not inconsiderable, so it is advisable to leave this work to a professional.

Tiling is another skilled job, best left to the professional where large areas are involved. The tiles must always be laid on a sound, firm base such as a concrete screed and fixed with a suitable waterproof adhesive. Remember that only fully vitrified tiles can be used outside, and, if in doubt, check with your supplier.

Above: **A serene marble fountain, set upon a plinth of mosaic, dominates this Islamic-style courtyard. The colourful and detailed mosaic evokes the design of an exotic Arabian carpet.**

Right: **Here decorative tiles have been used to provide relief to this concrete screen.**

Opposite: **Silver lustre mosaic tiles shimmer in reflection in this exotic stylized fountain.**

new materials

Creating a garden is a vibrant and exhilarating process, one that is active in the present and emerging from, rather than fixed on, ideas from the past. As the garden is part of the human environment, it follows that fashions there will keep pace with other areas of life. Developments in technology bring with them new design styles and materials, and the garden is an ideal stage on which to create fun, surprise or even shock.

Left: **Startling design concepts are always to be found at the annual Chaumont Garden Festival in France. This sweeping tunnel, formed from hoops of thin plastic film, creates vibrant effects of colour and light that change with the sun.**

modern materials

Plastics have in the past been associated with shoddiness, but they have now totally outgrown that derelict image through production techniques that have developed products of amazing technical sophistication and versatility.

"Plastic" is a generic term that refers to a huge range of materials. They can be soft, bendable, rigid or liquid, transparent, opaque, translucent, coloured, patterned, processed into textiles and paints or moulded into shapes, to suit whatever purpose is required. Those most relevant to garden use include Perspex (Plexiglas), which can be moulded into solid shapes or flat sheets, and polycarbonate, a lightweight alternative that is more scratch-resistant and is suitable for glazing. Polypropylene can be injection moulded and was made famous in the 1960s by Robin Day's stacking chairs, which have now become an integral part of everyday life. Teflon is best known for its use as a non-stick lining for kitchenware, but it can also be used as a waterproofing coating for textiles. The end products are immensely practical, being lightweight, waterproof and weather resistant. Fears about colour fading and surface deterioration are largely outdated. Modern plastics always tend to look new, which is perhaps not always desirable in the garden.

Rubber is a natural material that is beginning to make an appearance outside. Its main benefit is its soft, yielding quality, making it much in demand for children's play areas. Its high cost and scarcity has led to the development of interesting synthetic alternatives. Synthetic rubber sheet with a raised stud profile is a useful, non-slip floor covering for terraces and play spaces.

Astroturf is recognized as a tough, low-maintenance sports surface and is now beginning to appear in small gardens where natural lawns are inappropriate. Popular with both children and parents, it provides a fresh green surface that can withstand any amount of wear and tear, or simply look green all year round with the minimum of attention.

Below: **This design is based on a section through a plant stem. Vertical rubber pipes represent the vessels through which water and nutrients flow, while tall wire mesh cylinders give support for young succulents. Rubber particles represent the soil.**

Above: **Here plastic-covered wooden garden hoes dominate a section of this garden, providing a humorous wave of colour.**

Right: **Translucent "bubble effect" Perspex columns provide visually neutral support for the curved plastic "wave" canopy and inject a sense of graceful movement to the underwater theme.**

boundaries and screens

The type of boundary you choose for a space depends on several factors: opaque boundaries provide privacy while translucent ones give protection from the wind without blocking the view; an opening or arch can be sited to frame a focal point.

Opposite: **The steel frame of this screen is inset with an acrylic panel laminated with reflective film to create a cool, shimmering surface.**

Below: **This sail-like canopy provides welcome shelter from the sun.**

Transparency is one of the greatest qualities of Perspex (Plexiglas), making it ideal wherever separation is required without blocking out light or view. Clear Perspex is shatter-resistant and tough, and it is often used in place of toughened glass to screen a balcony from wind, though the benefits of lighter weight and easier handling must be offset against its vulnerability to scratching. However, it is in its brilliant colours that Perspex comes into its own as a decorative material. Possessing the qualities of stained glass without its fragility, it can be clear and jewel-like or opaque and mysterious.

Endlessly exciting graphic effects can be achieved using panels cut from clear or coloured sheet material. Geometric shapes can be used as insets to relieve a plain rendered wall or set along the top of the wall in adjoining panels. In a large garden, where there is sufficient space, monolithic panels can be fixed into the ground like glowing sentinels, to capture the effects of moving sunlight.

A courtyard can be brought to life after dark with a huge vertical light box. A number of small, coloured light boxes can even be incorporated into an open slatted timber screen to enliven a sheltered seating space.

A sense of discovery is desirable in even the smallest garden. A screen is a valuable device to foil an opening or bring an element of seclusion to a covered dining area. You could make a lively retro curtain, reminiscent of a clinking, Courrèges frock, by connecting small discs of Perspex with metal rings and hanging it to screen off a private part of the garden.

Simple screening effects can be achieved by stretching synthetic textiles across a timber framework. This versatile system, which can be made up of individual panels, is useful in urban locations and exposed areas, such as roof terraces. The textiles can be fixed vertically, diagonally or horizontally to provide privacy or shelter from sun and wind. For a less formal solution, a sail-like canopy makes an effective shield from the weather and a good privacy barrier, with the triangular shape providing a sweeping dynamic. It can be slung from a wall and stretched tight with ropes tied to bolts in the ground.

organic

The constraints and pressures of daily life, with its very tight schedules, cramped commuting and the stressful effect of being subject to constant noise, can lead to a desire to opt out entirely from the rat race. This is seldom practicable, but at least at home in the garden it is possible to react against the norm and create a restorative refuge, where nature rules and organic forms and materials are dominant.

Left: **In a wonderful example of freedom of organic expression, a seething mass of young shoots, in the guise of teaspoons, pushes up the earth to reach daylight, while a boardwalk entices the onlooker to investigate the hidden depths.**

Freestyle

A lateral approach to using materials in the garden can open up a wealth of unusual creative possibilities, leading to fantastical abstract art and an altered perception of common features.

Opposite: **Natural materials lend themselves readily to sculptural devices. Slung across an overgrown pond on lengths of fishing net, this "bridge" is draped with a seething tangle of weed-infested sisal, looking like an escaped sea monster.**

By relaxing ideas about form and structure, it is possible to make a pleasingly unconventional, untamed garden, using natural, unfinished materials that, instead of being arranged along conventional lines, are allowed to follow their own rhythm and shape. In this wilder, less restrictive kind of garden, birds and insects can find havens for nesting among twigs and vines, with watering holes nearby for refreshment. The calming and introspective effect extends to humans, too, of course, and there should be space for generous rustic seating and fascinating sculptural effects.

Right: **Driftwood is piled high to form a textural rustic pillar.**

Right: **A rusty old rail truck provides the perfect backdrop to tufts of free-flowing golden grasses.**

It is always interesting to interpret conventional design ideas using materials that are normally associated with an entirely different use. A funky, contemporary interpretation might contrast organic materials with a very strict, modern design. This kind of garden can take an off-beat theme, and might utilize unexpected materials for constructions, as well as incorporating quirky decorative details made from so-called "found objects".

With a lateral mind and an eye for shape and texture, a whole world of reclaimed materials can be re-created into sculptural forms, which are all the more pleasing for the release of personal inventiveness they can inspire. Driftwood provides rich pickings, often taking on surprising anthropomorphic forms that can be incorporated into themed set-pieces. It is also well worth keeping your eyes open near construction sites for the possibility of useful pieces of construction materials. Generous slabs of timber, such as old house beams, make excellent building blocks. Clearance sales and classified advertisements can also yield booty, such as old factory floors and disused railway sleepers (ties). Specialist reclamation dealers are always a good source of unusual building materials. Though often pricey, they offer the advantages of a wide choice and the facility to deliver to site.

groundwork

Making one's way through an organic garden should feel like a textural exploration, with timber boardwalks pushing their way through wild grasses and logs bridging gushing streams as if they have simply fallen into place.

Right: **Rusting metal washers can be used to add textural detail to a small area of floor.**

Below: **Horizontal sections sliced through an old tree trunk make a sympathetic rustic pathway through the garden planting.**

Wild landscapes demand an informal trail rather than a paved path. Rough planks make a textural surface that contrasts well with fresh green grass and is both stylish and easy to walk on. For a natural effect, range pieces of different sizes and shapes in an irregular, flowing pattern that moves with the contours of the land. A meandering path of circular log slices is an alternative, creating the effect of stepping-stones. The timbers, treated with preservative, can be positioned directly in the ground, though it is preferable to use gravel or compacted hardcore as a base. Ensure that the surface of the wood lies beneath the height of mower blades so the area can be maintained easily.

Chipped bark makes a cheap surfacing for paths and helps to suppress weeds. Its dark brown colour is natural and unobtrusive and it is light and easy to handle. Heavy, woven jute or sisal, normally sold for interior carpeting, is a possibility in areas of light traffic. It makes an interesting contrast with planting and will also suppress weeds. When it eventually rots down, it can be covered with a new layer.

Aggregates such as chippings and pebbles can be used for surfacing. Think laterally about industrial and domestic leftovers too, such as metal washers, steel filings or broken terracotta. Success lies in the presentation, so arrange them like works of art, not garbage.

Opposite: **Free-form design needs to be safe: this attractively haphazard walkway of random planks and posts is firmly footed into concrete foundations.**

raised beds and steps

A series of terraces can add enormous visual and spatial appeal to tricky sites such as long, narrow gardens or those with steep slopes. Raised beds add a vertical dimension to small gardens and allow cultivation where soil levels are low.

Right: **Railway sleepers (ties) make effective steps in this small courtyard garden.**

Below: **Large round wooden poles form a retaining wall to this raised bed.**

Both raised beds and terraces require retaining walls. These can be costly to build in brick or stone, but in an organic treatment, where the look should be informal and freer, they can be achieved simply with very effective results.

Whole sections of young tree trunks, with their irregularities of shape and texture, look very much part of the landscape. They can be arranged horizontally to contain a low bed but are perhaps best lined up vertically to create retaining walls. Specialist timber merchants can supply them, but if sourcing proves difficult, round poles sold for fencing posts can be used.

Railway sleepers (ties) are very versatile and their rectilinear shape aids construction. They can be hard to cut and because they are very heavy they must have good concrete foundations; steel bolts and ties give additional security. They may be stacked horizontally for a shallow bed, but set on end, side by side, sections of sleepers make sturdy retaining walls.

Rustic-style steps can be created by using heavy sections of timber for the risers. Sleepers provide well-proportioned, ready-to-go "building blocks", while whole round, rustic logs do a similar job, though slightly more informally. These are perhaps best used to retain a shallow flight of deep steps, which can be surfaced with contrasting gravel or chipped bark.

Opposite: **A raised boardwalk is an excellent way to navigate a wild or wet garden. Ensure that the timber is strong enough to take the weight of traffic, and set it securely in concrete footings.**

boundaries and screens

The natural texture required for informal fencing can be achieved using one of the new woven materials, which may be purchased by the roll. Alternatively, you could weave a screen of reeds or bamboo, or plant fresh willow withies.

Below: **Screening need not block a view, but can serve merely as a delineation of space. Here, rustic poles act as supports for the steel wires that surround the beds almost invisibly.**

Fencing on a roll is cheap and versatile. Made from heather, reed or split bamboo, securely woven together with wire, its understated appearance blends subtly into the background. It combines exceptionally well with informal planting and also makes very good lightweight screening for roof terraces and balconies, where it is an efficient diffuser for wind and sunshine.

Heavy woven hurdles are made following an ancient craft tradition that is currently undergoing a revival in new rustic gardens. In various sizes, they consist of willow withies woven through a strong framework of hazel uprights. They are expensive but are beautifully finished, sometimes woven into different patterns. Cheaper, more rustic versions are woven with split hazel. Some craftsmen will undertake special commissions for custom designs to be built on site, but before investing too much, it is worth remembering that the lifespan of these materials is only a few years.

Alternatively, you can plant a "living willow" fence, which will continue to grow as a permanent feature, sprouting fresh leaves each spring. You simply push freshly cut withies diagonally into the ground and weave them together into a firm framework. Maintenance is minimal: just a clip in autumn to keep them in shape. Fresh withies can be bought at shows in early spring or ordered directly from a grower.

All kinds of dried materials suitable for making into boundary features are available. Slim golden reeds, bought from thatching specialists, can be tied into bundles to make elegant Japanese-style screens. Bamboo canes are available in a variety of heights and thicknesses for making rigid screens and plant supports; join them with carefully made matching knots tied at the crossing points. Flexible willow is sometimes available grown from different species that yield purple, orange or yellow stems to add a coloured dimension to a design. The stems can be woven through tall hazel sticks to make screens and fences.

Above: **In a new take on the garden washing line, this very effective curtain screen is made from hundreds of wooden clothes pegs.**

Far left: **Corn cobs, sandwiched between wire mesh, screen a cotton-lined walkway.**

Left: **Bales of hay, surrounded by reinforced glass provide unusual bench structures.**

structures

Free up your mind and think Robinson Crusoe. With little more than a tangle of vines, some pieces of driftwood and a vivid imagination, you can create a fantastical structure that will please you and all the local wildlife that visits your garden.

String and rope made from natural hemp have gorgeous textural qualities and make wonderful aids to organic construction. Adults and children alike will appreciate a simple swing made from lengths of stout rope knotted through holes at each end of a good, smooth wooden plank and hung from a thick branch. A pergola would provide support where a tree is not available.

Rope ladders, made by knotting together rungs of thick dowelling, can be suspended from a tree or wall and used as jungle-inspired supports for vines. Ropes knotted into nets make organic boundaries or screens, plant trainers and hammocks, or could form part of a climbing frame in a children's adventure area.

Above: **Ancient trees provide an excuse to rig up a simple rope swing on which to while away the hours.**

Left: **An attractive inhabited dovecote introduces an air of romance and intimacy to the garden.**

Above: **Gabions, normally associated with civil engineering, seem to have become synonymous with new garden design. These, filled with attractive flint cobbles, have been cleverly incorporated into the arbour structure to form a seating area and raised planters.**

A garden retreat is a more permanent structure, whether it is completely enclosed or an open-sided shelter. It can be anything from a studio, in which to write or paint, to a potting shed or a place to entertain. The best hideaways look as if they have been there forever, whatever their purpose. For the forester look, a framework cut from wind-damaged trees and clad with split logs would make a good basic shell, to which a shady veranda supported by branched tree trunks could be added. Roof it with overlapping shingles – small discs or rectangles of sawn timber – or try a reed or brushwood thatch.

For real "outback" style, finish the walls with mismatched, faded planks and make the roof from discarded sheets of corrugated metal. Any combination of driftwood, woodland cuttings, sawn softwood, twisted vines and ropes will do. Really, anything goes when creating such a playhouse – make it just as wild as you like. The only proviso is that it should be safely and sturdily constructed, and be wind- and watertight. On the other hand, however untamed it looks on the surface, there is no reason why it should not be fitted with every modern convenience inside: heating, lighting, even water and cooking facilities. A shaded veranda outside, with a barbecue and a swing seat, will complete a retreat designed to invite you to stray into the garden.

Organic modernists could choose rudimentary hi-tech and build a retreat from gabions filled with oversized stones. Though rigid in form, the mass of stone has a raw, compelling attraction that suggests contained energy and nature exposed.

water

Water brings life to the world and demands a place in the natural garden for the sake of all the creatures living there. Whether you have space for a huge pond or just a shallow bowl, abundant wildlife will quickly be attracted to the garden to use it.

Opposite: **This naturalistic pond is carefully sited to link the garden with the glorious coastal landscape beyond.**

Below: **Weathered timbers set in sand and gravel give a gentle approach to the water's edge.**

Informal water features such as ponds, streams and waterfalls fit perfectly into an organic theme, but setting them in a natural landscape requires a sensitive touch. They need some sort of border and an approach from the rest of the garden. An appealing walkway can be made with weathered driftwood in a bed of smooth pebbles, and a shallow beach of loose stones allows birds to reach the water's edge. There are many other ways of incorporating charismatic pieces of timber in a water garden. A heavy board or split log bridge can span a small stream to connect different parts of the garden. A pontoon platform of planks overhanging a large pond is a great spot to sit. For security, it should be supported on posts bedded into a concrete base during the pond construction.

Water features can be constructed relatively simply with a flexible liner and pump. A gently bubbling spring spouting through pebbles is a lovely device where space is limited, set in a quiet spot where birds can gather. It can be run by a small submersible pump in a water reservoir in the form of a plastic garbage bin sunk in the ground. A layer of pebbles, through which the water emerges, is supported by a sheet of steel mesh. An extended area of pebbles spread around it naturalizes the effect, especially when combined with simple marginal plants such as variegated grasses and iris.

More ambitious schemes such as ponds and streams require planning to ensure the right balance of water, pump and reservoir. Black PVC liners are easy to handle and economically priced, though professionals specify more expensive butyl for its strength and flexibility under all conditions. Pumps may be submersible or housed above ground. They divide into those designed to power fountains or waterfalls and those capable of handling solids, which are required to work filtration systems in ponds. Large schemes should be professionally installed, though water features need not be ambitious to be successful and are great fun to make. However, outdoor electrical installations require special care, and it is prudent to appoint a qualified tradesman to make the connections.

the elements

Landscaping and garden design are exacting disciplines incorporating many layers of technical and artistic knowledge. These include horticulture, construction, history, ecology, fine art and spatial design. Creating the link and balance between these areas requires careful thought and judgement, and, as we have demonstrated, even the tiniest yard will benefit from special attention to detail.

Having seen a range of different garden styles, you may now feel that you have sufficient information to decide on your personal garden style; you may even have considered the planting and prepared a design plan. Once that is done, you can concentrate on all those detailed elements that, when brought together, complete the overall picture.

Researching suppliers, choosing objects and dreaming up special effects is a time-consuming business, and the information in this book should help you to short-cut some avenues by analysing the possibilities. A selection of suppliers and sources is included on pages 250–251. This is a creative area where you can have lots of fun, and we try to make it as interesting as possible for you.

Structural installations combine practical, architectural and decorative roles; by making the most appropriate decision about their design, your garden will have greater impact and become more enjoyable. The spatial contribution of steps, bridges and vertical structures are discussed and an examination of the

Left: **The use of architectural foliage gives immense presence to this Japanese-style courtyard, combining well with the substantial timber decking and the wooden pergola. The yellow parasol is echoed by the yellow flowering spikes of ligularias. This is an excellent example of how sophisticated attention to detailing can make all the difference to the look.**

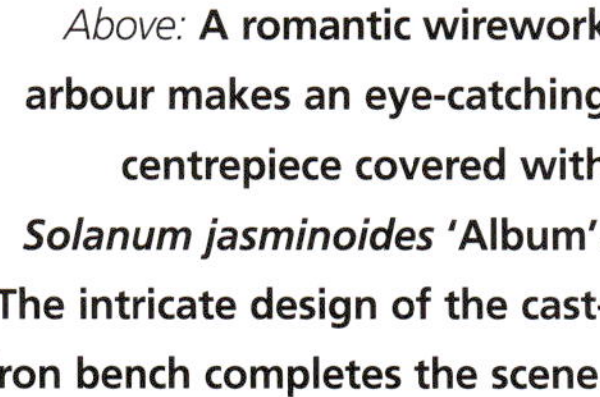

Above: **A romantic wirework arbour makes an eye-catching centrepiece covered with *Solanum jasminoides* 'Album'. The intricate design of the cast-iron bench completes the scene.**

Above right: **A flight of ancient steps is defined by the planting of pelargoniums. The alcoves of statuary provide visual relief and lead the eye to the terrace above.**

appropriate materials made. The contribution of pattern and texture when laying paving and tiling is covered. The designs and materials suitable for furniture and containers are assessed, to enable you to make fitting choices.

There is currently a fast-developing interest in the role of sculpture in the garden, with new galleries and parks opening all the time. This exciting and complex area is covered in some depth, with many photographs of exciting contemporary work that you can view and acquire. However, should you feel the creative urge to make your own piece, ways are suggested for you to reconstruct found or recycled objects. The horticultural artist is catered for as well, with ideas for plant training and still-life.

A broad range of exciting projects, from the very simple to some requiring a little more expertise, has been specially commissioned from a variety of talented artists, using a variety of different materials, from willow to wood, from metal to mosaic tiles. Full details of the materials and tools that are needed for these projects are set out with the method of construction. You will surely take a great deal of inspiration from these and endeavour to recreate some of them, or you may prefer to use them as a basis for your own individual interpretation.

paving patterns

Top right: **Alternate bands of sawn timber and pebbles are simple to lay and make a striking pathway through this timber pergola walk.**

Below right: **Black river pebbles laid on edge boldly centralize a mixed media design of pebbles, stone and brick, creating a change of texture within a foliage planting design.**

Below: **Concrete paviours meander across a sward, making a visual connection between the main house and the guest suite, without interrupting the natural flow of the garden.**

Bottom right: **A sensitive placing of brick paving enhances the softness and movement of this perennial border. Mortar between the bricks is omitted to allow self-seeding, which further naturalizes the effect.**

The function of paving in the garden is much more than simply providing a surface on which to walk. Paving can be likened to the floor and carpet of an interior room. Inside, flooring is chosen to complement wall coverings, curtains and furniture; outside, it must work with the architectural style of the house and its materials, the garden boundaries and planting. The feel of it under foot is important; is it smooth or lumpy, slippery or safe? Can furniture be placed on it without wobbling?

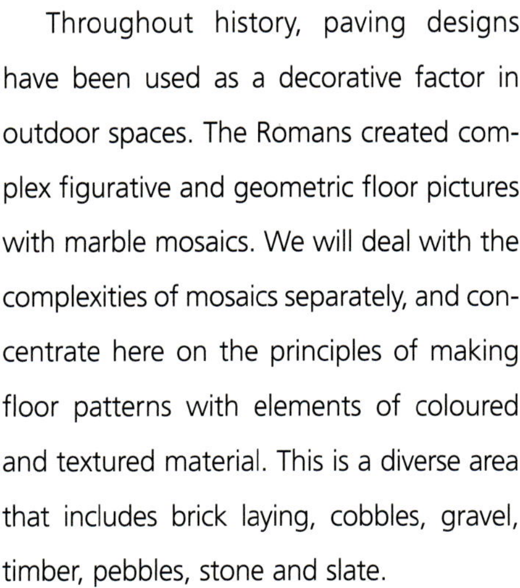

Its form is strategic to the overall plan and holds the complete picture together. An eclectic garden can be transformed by the unifying effect of a plain paving format, while a clipped topiary style would be enlivened by a clever pattern or texture.

Paths also have an important directional function, leading you through the various experiences of the garden. Terraces are gathering places to meet up with friends and family, places to sit or entertain.

Throughout history, paving designs have been used as a decorative factor in outdoor spaces. The Romans created complex figurative and geometric floor pictures with marble mosaics. We will deal with the complexities of mosaics separately, and concentrate here on the principles of making floor patterns with elements of coloured and textured material. This is a diverse area that includes brick laying, cobbles, gravel, timber, pebbles, stone and slate.

The choice of construction material will determine the type of effect that can be achieved, together with its suitability for its purpose. It would be pointless to lay

expensive York stone in a wild garden, and in any case it would look totally out of place. In the same way, timber railway sleepers would look absurd with a period town house. Hard-wearing constituents like granite or cast concrete should be chosen where traffic is heavy, while gravels and cobbles are more suitable for areas where maintenance is not a major consideration.

The shape of the paving material controls the type of design that can be produced. One of the most versatile and easy to obtain is moulded clay brick, which can be sourced in a good range of colour tones, from reddish to grey-black. The rect-angular shape lends itself to a multitude of combinations, and the colour tones can be introduced as part of the design. They can be laid in straight lines, at right angles and zigzags; laid lengthways or combined with insets of the short end face. A single line of a dark brick can form a decorative border to a path of another material such as stone.

Left: **Positive channels of red brick cut through a riven stone path to emphasize the direction towards the steps in the garden beyond. An inspired border of eucomis boldly reinforces the statement and a red brick plinth for the distant urn completes the intended effect.**

Below left: **Timber decking is the natural accompaniment for this summerhouse in a seaside garden. Straight lengths of board laid widthways provide a sense of movement.**

High-fired engineering bricks are the most suitable for paving because they are very hard, strong and will not absorb moisture. Their slightly shiny, technical appearance normally lends itself to a formal situation, and the darkest purple-blacks can look elegant in a modern setting, perhaps combined with black slate. Softer, hand-made bricks are not usually recommended for paving, but their mellow qualities make them ideal for some traditional settings. As the bricks age, mosses tend to grow between them, lending a weathered air. Where possible, avoid cheap bricks, which are neither practical nor attractive.

Above: **Clay facing bricks are not really strong enough for use in paving, but they do lend a charmingly informal air to this cottage garden, complementing the materials as well as the age of the building.**

Left: **In large gardens, it is often inappropriate or too expensive to lay paving. Grass crisply defines and formalizes this island bed, while clear stretches of gravel provide the "white space".**

Above: **Changes of level are easily accommodated by the use of timber decking. Clean lines and restrained planting combine to create a tranquil pool area, linking a wooden terrace with the main garden.**

Below: **The herringbone arrangement of bricks makes a lively, yet informal, directional link through gravel in this romantic-style garden. The path leads enticingly to a well-tended lawn.**

Clay and terracotta tiles are the other popular pressed forms of paving material. Colours range from pale sand to bright red, depending on the source and firing method. In cold climates, ensure that they are fired at high temperatures to withstand frost and have them laid professionally to avoid cracking and breaking up.

York and other sandstones, limestone, granite and slate are gorgeous but costly. The beauty of natural materials is their variable colour, their patina and texture, which often shows mineral and fossil strata. They can be finished in different ways to change their appearance or performance and will mellow with age and use.

Sandstone and slate can be sawn into rectangular slabs, which gives them a very smooth surface while revealing the layers of colour tones within; in this form they suit fine architecture, both contemporary and classical. Alternatively, they can be split, leaving them with an irregular surface and edges resulting in paving with a less structured, somewhat ancient appearance.

Granite is one of the hardest-wearing minerals, and rectangular setts are one of the most popular ways of cutting forms for paving. These rectangular pieces are usually set end-on in concrete to reveal a roughly surfaced square. Straight lines, diagonals or fans are the usual laying format, although their size and shape allow them to be arranged in circles. They also make good detailing features when combined with roundish materials like pebbles and cobbles.

Where budget is a consideration, it would be advisable to consider some of the better cast concrete replicas. Although some dreadful versions do exist, it is possible to source excellent versions of York paving, granite setts and terracotta tiles. You might be tempted by one of the aggregate mixes, which combine sophisticated textures and colours with excellent durability.

Concrete can be laid *in situ*, and if you have an artistic bent, you might like to experiment further with textures, patterns and eccentric aggregates. Concrete is supremely versatile and may be mixed with almost anything.

Informal and woodland situations provide an opportunity to experiment with timber. Horizontally sawn logs make great stepping stones through grass, and long sections of timber like railway sleepers (ties) can be butted up next to each other, perhaps with fine stones or chipped bark as infill between them.

Above: **The laminated texture of slate makes it suitable for using in wild, naturalistic designs. These borders are created from irregular pieces of slate, arranged vertically, whereas they are laid flat to form the surface of the path.**

Below: **Curves place special demands on the garden designer; the spaces around these square, brick shapes are filled in with an array of pebbles. The result is an interesting contrast of form and texture.**

steps

A sloping site can be a visual asset, but must be made manageable with terracing and changes of levels to enable circulation and easy cultivation. Conversely, a flat landscape can seem dull, and it may be desirable to excavate and landfill to create new shallows and mounds that will enliven the overall aesthetic. The practical way to move between these levels is by flights of steps. These should be thought of as not merely practical, but as making a sensory contribution to the design and interest of the garden. Steps emphasize dimension and scale while incorporating texture and architectural effects.

Steps can add mystery because the ultimate destination may be out of sight. In a woodland situation, they might rise to reveal a clearing containing a sun-dappled pond with fish swimming lazily beneath the surface, or a sculpture positioned to surprise. In a topiary garden, they could lead down to a high-hedged parterre enclosing a secret seat or a fountain.

Steps can take a dynamic role in a garden, leading to an important focal point or entrance. A grand flight of stone steps could descend from a classical balustraded terrace to a formal garden below; at the front of a town house, steps might guide the way to the entrance door, framed with clipped box trees in tubs. Natural stones such as granite or certain tough slates would be appropriate materials, and the surface should be textured to avoid slipping. Sandstones in their pale, mellow shades are always attractive, though less hard-wearing.

Above: **Informal landscapes demand subtly defined treatments. Mossy stone steps wind haphazardly up this wooded slope, taking care to integrate well with their surroundings.**

Above right: **Dark tree trunks, accentuated by the white gravel, form the risers of this slightly formalized woodland stairway. The carefully placed rocks fix the eye to a border of dramatic boulders on the right-hand side, asymmetrically balanced on the left by low evergreen shrubs.**

Brick, which can be laid in a variety of patterns, also lends itself to formal designs, both traditional and contemporary. Durable engineering bricks that are hard enough to withstand wear and weathering should be selected. Available in burnished colours ranging from deep purple/red through to darkest grey/black, they make a handsome choice.

Practical and inexpensive, when concrete is laid *in situ* with care and attention to the finish, it is clean and functional and may be a good solution where lots of steps are needed on a limited budget.

In a small garden, it is likely that steps between levels will not have to travel very far, but every element has to work hard aesthetically. Turn a necessity into an interesting feature with three or four steps that are low, but wide and deep, to result in a gentle progression that has great presence.

Extended in scale, this style also works well over a long, shallow slope, with a series of shallow risers giving an elegant, gradual passage. The choice of material will entirely control the finished look: cool and sophisticated when made from smooth, sawn sandstone, or rustic and informal with risers of timber railway sleepers (ties) retaining treads covered in gravel or chipped bark. This design can be further emphasized by placing identical planted pots at the same end of each step.

Small gardens depend on the vertical dimension to extend their space, so a run of wooden steps could lead to a raised terrace of timber decking. This could be sited with access from windows in the house, or to create a sitting space over storage sheds.

Left: **Architectural planting can transform the simplest stairway. This steep rise of grey stone steps is controlled by the bordering pyramids of blue-green conifer, and framed by an overflowing swathe of deep mauve *Ceanothus impressus*.**

Below left: **The imaginative use of materials enables the designer to create interesting effects. To create these rounded steps, the risers are formed from bricks set on end, with treads of tiles laid on edge.**

Above: **Sawn timber slats retain compacted earth steps covered with fine pea shingle. The bold borders of frothy lady's mantle (*Alchemilla mollis*) make an idea foil for this simple scheme.**

Left: **These red brick steps are defined by a row of matching terracotta pots beside a wall of Virginia creeper (*Parthenocissus quinquefolia*), contrasted with the lime-green variegated helichrysum.**

tiles and mosaics

A splash of colour can bring focus to a feature that might otherwise be mundane; when combined with a textural element, it gives the feature added life. Mosaics bring these two assets together, involving the creation of a tapestry from small pieces of coloured or textured material bedded into cement. The usual materials are tiles of glazed ceramic, glass, terracotta, mirror or marble, or broken pieces of any of these. The versatile nature of these materials makes them suitable for a variety of objects.

Taking inspiration from these ideas, it is easy to see how addictive this craft can be, though it is best used judiciously unless you live in a sunny climate that can carry brilliant colour. Our project on page 198–201 shows how mosaics can be used in a subtle way to bring a new dimension to a practical object. Makeovers like this can be made with many familiar items: old pots can be turned into new planters, while drinking glasses take on a new image as lanterns transmitting light through coloured glass tiles.

Above: **Effective designs can be made using inexpensive broken tiles.**

Above right: **The Romans were great protagonists of the use of mosaic in architectural design, providing inspiration for artists throughout the last millennium. This faithful reproduction depicts sea creatures using tiny pieces of marble and stone. Though they swim around a classical water feature, it is interesting to note how casually contemporary they look.**

The legendary Spanish architect Gaudí famously used mosaics to cover strangely amorphic shapes over buildings in Barcelona. Wildly curving balconies, chimney pots resembling warriors' helmets and curious mushrooms, all became his subjects. At his landscape development, Parc Güell, a courtyard meeting place is dominated by a long, snaking bench, aptly named the serpentine seat, which is covered over every surface with broken fragments of multi-coloured ceramics.

Try building a sculpture from chicken wire and cement. An exotic creature would be fun, perhaps a crocodile covered with multi-coloured scales. Three-dimensional objects may be quite demanding, but it is easy to create stylized pictures of birds or animals on a wall or to enliven a pool surround with tropical fish.

Mosaic can, of course, take on an ordered mantle more suited to quiet, formal situations. Examples can still be seen of Roman floor mosaics. There are countless

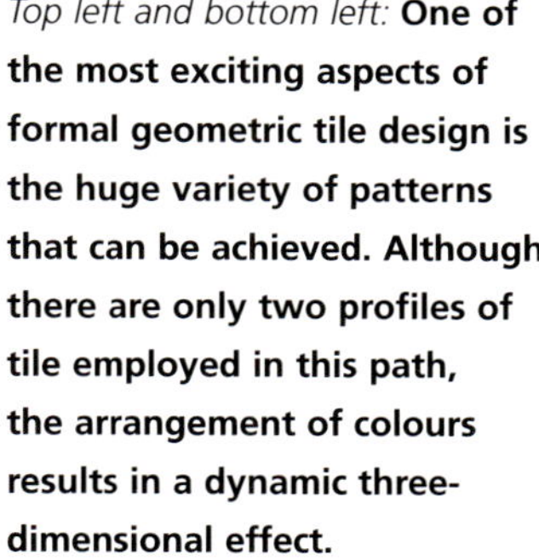

Top left and bottom left: **One of the most exciting aspects of formal geometric tile design is the huge variety of patterns that can be achieved. Although there are only two profiles of tile employed in this path, the arrangement of colours results in a dynamic three-dimensional effect.**

Left: **The balance of shape and colour controls mosaic design. Curious "push-me-pull-you" forms are framed by a background of cream shades.**

combinations of geometric forms, all based on the square, rectangle and triangle, which, according to their arrangement, result in linear, rectangular and circular patterns. By varying the medium, sophisticated results can encompass the understated pale tones of marble to black slate and burnt terracotta.

The influence of North Africa created Moorish Spain, with its palaces in Seville and Córdoba and the legendary Alhambra in Granada. Glazed tiles in geometric patterns composed of a kaleidoscope of deep greens, blues, reds and yellows seem to cover every surface. In Portugal, tiles are used to cover the walls and floors of avenues, steps and even the lining of canals. In most gardens this would be overwhelming, so isolate small sections to reflect the image. A flight of concrete steps could be transformed by setting glazed tiles into the face of the risers; complete the Mediterranean effect with a succession of geranium-filled pots at each level.

Above centre: **The small size and random shape of mosaic pieces allow them to be used to cover odd-shaped objects. This parasol stand has been transformed from the mundane to become an elegant part of the garden detailing.**

Above right: **There are many ways to use mosaics, as this rustic arbour shows. The panel depicting a flowering climber clearly demonstrates the subtle variations of colour possible when using glass as a medium.**

words and inscriptions

The carved inscription is understated and somewhat secret: it does not jump out but waits to be discovered. It can be provocative, propounding perhaps a philosophical idea or presenting a mathematical theory. It can be reassuring, extracting a meaningful line of poetry, or induce a smile with a frivolous remark. A memorial can mark an anniversary, evoking images of friends and family, or commemorate heroic deeds and landmark events.

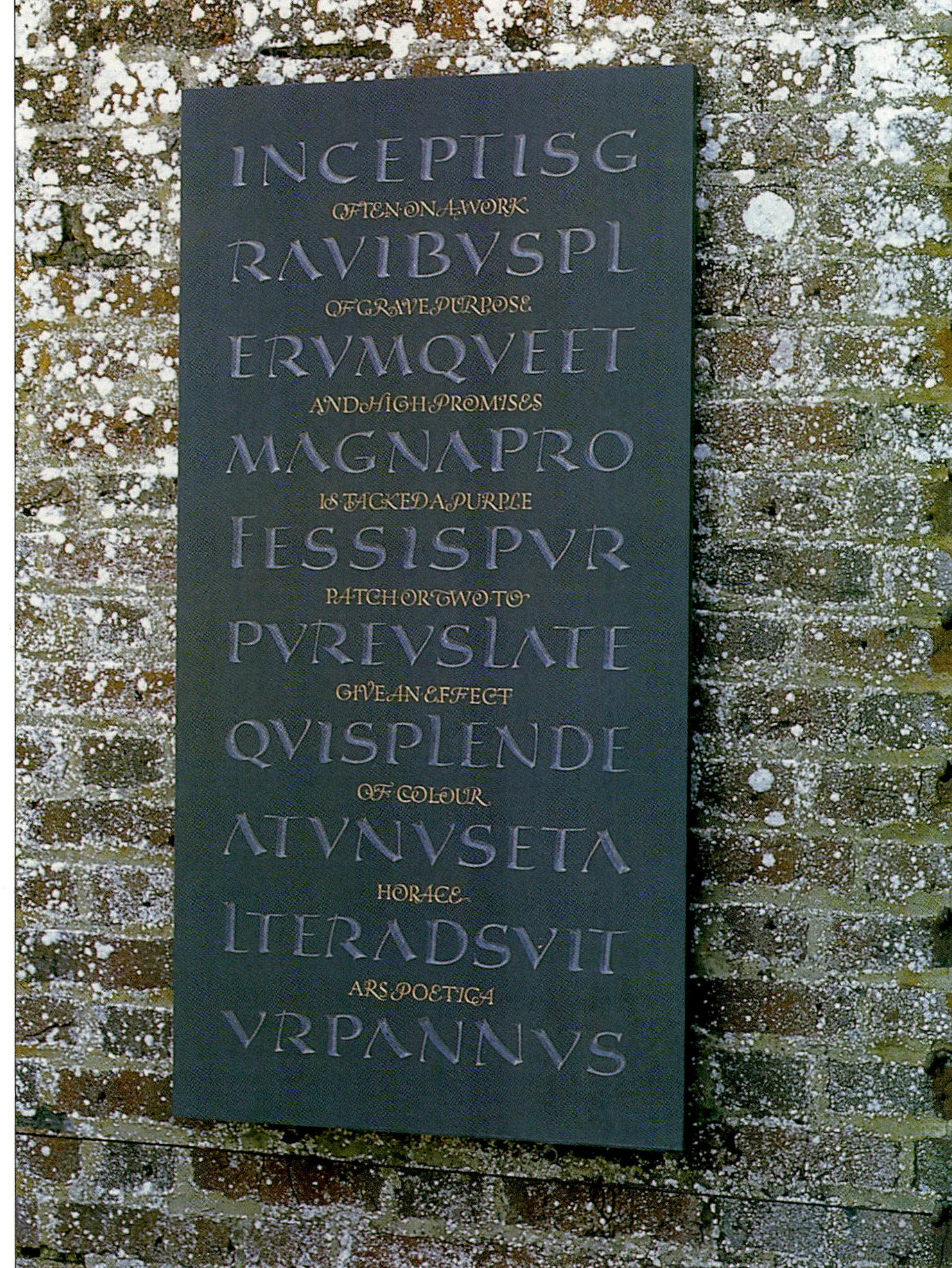

Sculpture can take many forms, and the success of this subtle area is much dependent upon the quality of materials and the skill of the craftsman. Calligraphy is a most beautiful art which is fully developed when the choice of lettering style reflects the provenance of the inscription. The development of script has taken place over several centuries, each period and geographical location having an influence on the result. Whether whole poems or single thoughts are selected, a mathematical series or a simple house number, each gives an opportunity to test the understanding of the sculptor.

Minerals and stones from around the world have their own special qualities of colour, texture and density, and even individual pieces from the same source can show marked differences through the strata of which they are composed.

Above: **'Moonstone III' made from Penrhyn slate by Meical Watts.**

Left: **'Inceptis Gravibus' made from Welsh slate by Brenda Berman & Annet Stirling.**

Because the finished piece of work may be quite small, it presents an opportunity to select a really beautiful piece of stone with both visual and tactile qualities.

A piece of granite could take the form of a large beach pebble, pounded and smoothed to reveal its glistening mica; this might be picked up and stroked while its inscribed wisdom is pondered. A textured slate could be sliced to form a plaque for a wall, inscribed with a line of prose. A piece of limestone revealing tiny fossils, entrapped in a prehistoric age, might be articulated as a sundial, making an analogy with the passing of time.

Gardens are places to stimulate the senses and memories. How gratifying, then, to be reminded of a favourite poem while meandering through the garden. In the Scottish isles, Ian Hamilton-Finlay, a reclusive artist philosopher, has created a thought-provoking landscape, surprising visitors at watery vistas with architectural jetsam and rough-hewn stones. The siting and selection alone of these pieces is inspired, but when inscribed with thoughts and sayings, both disturbing and amusing, it becomes a holistic experience. So we see that inscribed pieces do not have to take a formal position. They can be settled in woodland or in a clump of bamboo, found nestling among grasses or placed beside a seat.

Stone is not a prerequisite, of course; when informality is more appropriate, concrete is ideal. Stepping stones cast at intervals through grass give an opportunity to tell a story; compose one and scratch it on the surface before the cement sets.

Below left: **'Initial Posts' made from Welsh slate by Martin Jennings.**

Below right: **'Found Letters' made from Portland stone by Alex Peever.**

Bottom left: **'Hermetic Numerals' made from Welsh slate by John Das Gupta.**

Bottom right: **'WB Yeats Table' made from Welsh blue/black slate and Derbyshire limestone by James Salisbury.**

The vertical elements of the garden are an important aspect of its visual framework. They provide balance by making the link between the garden and surrounding buildings or large trees, or alternatively they give vertical scale in a level landscape. They may be a purely architectural statement or also provide an opportunity to grow climbing plants; in both cases they introduce further layers of colour and texture in combinations of materials and finish, foliage and flowers.

decorative structures

Top right: **A storage place for tools need not be purely functional; this pretty octagonal hut has been integrated with the rest of the garden by a pergola from which to suspend hanging baskets. The flame-red nasturtiums contrast well with the pretty shades of blue and mauve of the woodwork.**

The most appropriate materials for the construction of a framework would be metal and timber. The advantage of metal is its physical strength combined with a very light visual appearance. Although today wrought iron really means steel, it can be formed into very elegant shapes, and intricate designs can be made from wirework over a steel frame. To be fully weatherproofed, steel must be galvanized before it is painted, but it is quite fashionable at the moment to leave it natural and rusty. This is fine, as long as the metal is of sufficient weight: a flimsy construction will fall apart.

Any large structure made from timber should be made from adequately sized sections. Hardwoods need the least maintenance, and the natural grain looks best if it is treated from time to time with varnish or oil. Pressure-treated softwoods are a cheaper alternative, but if painted will need regular maintenance. Preservative stains, which colour the wood without obliterating the texture, are an alternative.

In its grandest embodiment, this feature would be a free-standing arbour, perhaps

Above left: **A highly original lakeside pergola has been created on a concrete raft over the water. Constructed from wrought iron and glass, it encloses a metalwork throne.**

Left: **This romantic seating arbour is practically obscured by golden hop (*Humulus lupulus* 'Aureus') and a white rambling rose. Deep blue nepeta, which complements the mauve-stained woodwork, frames the picture with great style.**

making the focal point for a long vista. The romantically classical image is of twirling wrought iron or an intricate design in wood, painted in lilac blue or soft grey. However, it might also be formed in steel to make a contemporary temple, or in carved oak for a robust arts and crafts design.

A primarily architectural statement should be left unadorned, while a simpler framework would be ideal for climbers such as roses, clematis or passionflowers to complete the visual statement. If made large enough to enclose a table and chairs, it can combine a practical function, making an elegant location for lunch or aperitifs.

At its simplest, a seating arbour enclosed by trellis at the back, top and sides can be easily placed, even in a courtyard garden. Used to support jasmine and honeysuckle, it makes a perfumed resting place. Lots of timber versions are available, but it is also possible to create more delicate looking designs from fine metalwork.

Left: **An ebullient pair of silvery *Salix alba* var. *sericea*, trained into standards, is an inspired choice to frame this sentry-box-style arbour, just large enough to contain a chair. The frame, roof and trellis are made from timber that is painted a discreet blue-grey.**

Below left: **The birds have flown from this delicate Victorian wirework aviary, leaving it ready to be planted with a climber such as *Clematis orientalis* or *C. macropetala*.**

The arbour concept can be extended to that of a pergola, usually made from timber rafters supported on upright pillars. When attached to a house wall and erected over a terrace, a pergola clothed in climbers gives privacy and shade. Columns of steel or cast concrete make an elegant alternative support, where the architecture demands it. A less physically dominant effect can be achieved by stringing horizontal wires between walls; in this case, the plants have to do all the decorative work.

A free-standing pergola makes a gracious walkway to connect one area of the garden with another, or to frame a

Above: **This enchantingly romantic arbour, set in a wild flower meadow, has been created from a combination of cast and wrought iron.**

Left: **Climbing supports make attractive architectural features to stand alone or bring contrast to a border. This wooden tripod shows off the clematis flowers in all their full glory.**

prominent feature. It is also a great way to grow a variety of climbers, alternating the species at each pillar so that each one has enough space and air. Both physical and visual strength are essential for this sort of feature: flimsy structures do not work. Thoughtful design, appropriate materials and competent installation are crucial to achieve the right scale and to avoid movement or deterioration.

The planted tunnel is gaining popularity again. Basically, this is a series of connected curved arches lining a path. This device is probably best suited to a large garden where it can be enjoyed only when looking at its best. When space does not permit such a grand statement, a single arch can be a useful framing device. By focusing the eye, it can direct movement towards a path or make an entrance feature in the opening of a low hedge or perimeter fence. The rose arch is the ultimate romantic image, but there are other flowering climbers to choose from that are equally beautiful and much longer lasting. For a permanent effect, ivy (*Hedera*) is the obvious evergreen, but in mild climates, a wider choice of species is available.

The garden gate is also an effective decorative structure in its own right. Reclamation yards are a good source of redundant objects that can be given a new lease of life, so why not find a wrought-iron gate and then create an opening especially for it? A tall hedge is a good subject for treatment; even if there is no access to the adjacent land, the openwork quality of a gate allows a view through to the scenery beyond. It also suggests spaciousness by hinting that there is a further garden to explore. You may have the opposite scenario, say an existing wall with an opening. Instead of choosing a ready-made gate from a catalogue, take the opportunity to commission one from the growing corps of artist blacksmiths who can create a design especially for your garden.

The obelisk is an essentially simple vertical structure, and by this virtue can be extremely versatile. It can be made in any height, be adorned with ornamental finials, and take on the related forms of the cone, pyramid or column. Obelisks and pyramids can be sited singly to give height in a border, in pairs to

frame a pathway, and in even numbers to enclose a formal parterre. The pure shape of cones allows them to be arranged in groups of three, or asymmetrically in varying heights, resulting in a dynamic sculptural statement. Columns may carry a pergola, frame a doorway or support an urn or sculpture.

If beautifully designed, obelisks can stand unadorned and alone. However, if they are destined to support permanent climbing shrubs, they should be strongly made from durable materials like metal and timber. Where informality is more appropriate, such as in the kitchen garden, hazel and willow tepees make understated but adequate supports for peas, beans and annual flowers.

It is advisable, especially in a small garden, to consider practicalities like the storage of tools and compost (soil mix). This could take the form of a long, low wooden box with a liftable lid, lined with resin or zinc for protection against damp. When a foam cushion is laid on top, it doubles up as a bench. Developing the idea, you can make it a structural feature built from bricks to retain a planting bed. By turning a second "box" at right angles, a seating unit is formed. The lid is made from timber, and the resulting corner space is perfect for a feature plant. A rectangular table completes a unit that is economical with space and cost.

A shed can be an interesting garden feature as well as a vital storage space. It need not be a major investment: the most basic design can be made to look smart when painted creatively. Try a *trompe l'oeil* of branches and birds or some fake windows with scenes of the potting shed inside. Even a tiny sentry-box style would look dashing painted in vertical stripes of colour.

Where space allows, a larger building is a luxury. If robustly constructed and insulated, it would double as a studio or children's den. A shingled timber roof would lift it from the commonplace, and with the addition of a shady veranda it would become a haven from which to admire the efforts of the day. The concept of a basic shed has thus been transformed into a garden room, expanding the scope of your garden both physically and visually.

Left: **A Victorian-style gazebo sits romantically at this lakeside, the scene framed by scented *Philadelphus thalictrum*. White-painted basketwork chairs complement the intricate design of the timber trelliswork.**

Above right: **This elegant gate provides an enticing glimpse of the garden beyond.**

Right: **These simple, timber obelisks give structure and height to an informal border.**

Willow obelisks can be used as architectural features in their own right or placed in pots so that climbers can be trained up them. Obelisks also act as focal points, adding height and structure to beds and borders. For an evening extravaganza, you might even like to adorn the obelisk with fairy lights to create a highly original decoration.

willow obelisk

Materials and Equipment

3 grades of willow:

4 corner poles, 2000mm (78in) long and 18mm (¾in) in diameter

medium-grade willow for the sides, 13mm (½in) in diameter

thin pieces of willow for the twisted base and ball (about the thickness of a pencil)

willow clippings for the ball

pieces of wood for the support block

nails

hammer

drill

sharp knife

pair of secateurs (hand pruners)

chicken wire

pair of gloves

pair of pliers

linseed oil

white spirit (turpentine)

Preparation

Willow can be found in woods but it is advisable to check first if there are any restrictions on gathering material from local woods. A local wildlife trust or wood yard might also be able to supply you with material or at least advise you on where it can be obtained in your area. The willow comes in tied bundles which need to be soaked in the river so that they will be soft enough to work with. It should be soaked for one to two weeks, depending on the thickness of the wands and on the time of year, which will obviously affect the temperature of the water. If the bark falls off the willow when you work with it, then it has been soaked for too long. To test if the willow is pliable enough, twirl the tips around your finger several times. It should be soft enough to bend without cracking. If you do not have access to a stretch of water, you can also soak the willow in the bath tub. Drain the willow by standing the bundles up on one end.

1

1 Constructing a simple wooden support block, like the one shown here, makes working on the obelisk easier as well as more stable than working directly in the ground. Use leftover pieces of wood where possible. The dimensions of the block are 350 x 350 x 90mm (14 x 14 x 3½in). Drill holes as shown so that you can create obelisks of two sizes.

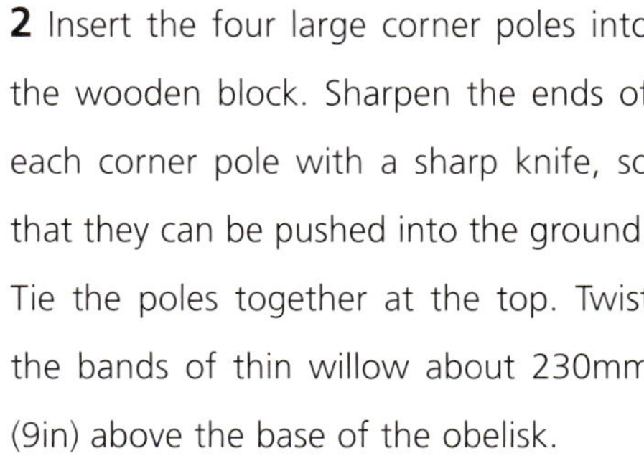

2 Insert the four large corner poles into the wooden block. Sharpen the ends of each corner pole with a sharp knife, so that they can be pushed into the ground. Tie the poles together at the top. Twist the bands of thin willow about 230mm (9in) above the base of the obelisk.

3 Nail the twisted willow base firmly in place at each of the corners.

2

3

4

4 Using a pair of secateurs (hand pruners), cut points at the ends of the medium-grade wands of willow, so that they can be pushed easily into the twisted base at the corners.

5 Push the wands into the twisted base at the corners and weave two wands up each side to form a criss-cross pattern.

6 To create the ball on top, scrunch up some willow clippings and carefully wrap a piece of chicken wire around them. The wire can be cut with a pair of pliers. It is advisable to wear gloves to protect your hands from any sharp pieces of wire.

7 Gently squash the ball on top of the obelisk, pushing the tails of the medium-grade willow wands into the ball to secure it firmly on top.

8 Using the thin willow wands, start weaving through and around the ball in order to cover over the netting. The willow is fairly pliable, so this process should be quite easy.

6

7

9 Continue threading the willow wands through and over the ball until none of the wire netting is showing. The finished obelisk can be treated with a mixture of boiled linseed oil and white spirit (in a ratio of 50:50) in order to improve its resistance to poor weather.

5

8

9

Right: **The finished obelisk can be used as a decorative focal point just as it is or festooned with annual climbers, such as sweet peas (*Lathyrus odoratus*), during the summer.**

garden furniture

Probably the first reason we place furniture in the garden is functional. A place to sit and a table to eat from are prerequisites. However, furniture plays a decorative role, too. A stylish bench, positioned at the end of a path, creates both an interesting picture and a reason to walk along to discover it; a tree seat further emphasizes the features of an important specimen.

Practicalities always have to be fully considered when working outdoors. If you plan to leave the furniture outside all year round, you must ensure that it is robust enough to withstand extremes of weather. The specification for the materials, construction and finish needs to be very different from that of pieces for interior use.

The most obvious choice of material for outdoor furniture is wood. It feels and looks naturally sympathetic since it was once alive itself. Suitable durable timbers include slow-growing teak and oak, iroko and red cedar, the first two being by far the most beautiful and expensive. However, due to the enormous upsurge of demand for garden products, there is an increasing number of hitherto unknown

Top (centre): **French-style, ironwork café furniture is a perennial favourite. Its visual fragility and formal appearance make it ideal for courtyards and terraces.**

Above: **Obviously comfortable and robust, these teak chairs can be left out in summer to gain an attractive, weathered patina and then folded away again in winter. The table is sturdy enough to stay outdoors all year round.**

Above: **A stylish "Adirondack" lounger looks completely at ease on this wooden deck. The ridged surface of the handsome pot echoes the prominent veining of surrounding vegetation and the rhythm of the stripes in the timberwork.**

Left: **This sensuous sculptural seating is made from solid bronze resin with a special surface finish.**

tropical hardwoods on the market. Do support the cause of conservation by buying only those timbers that can be guaranteed to come from licensed plantation sources.

Softwoods grow quickly, so are easily sustainable and more ecologically sound. But they do not have the same qualities of durability or appearance. To help them last, they can be finished with preservative stains or painted. These finishes result in furniture that is more superficially decorative than those made from natural woods.

Left: **This imaginative swing seat has stood the test of time, hanging in an apple tree.**

Below left: **Oak is one of the most beautiful and enduring timbers, acquiring a silvery patina with exposure to the weather. This elegantly curved bench demonstrates how good contemporary design can also be classical.**

Timber can swell and crack when saturated with water, so the design of wooden surfaces should be slatted so that water runs away, instead of collecting in pools. Tables, benches and chairs formed out of solid sections are likely to have problems with their joints if no drainage feature is incorporated.

In order to sustain lasting durability, wooden exterior furniture has tended to be quite heavy and bulky. Although it has an incomparable feel of comfort and substance, the size can be a drawback for small gardens. In response to demands for choice, there is now a good selection of folding timber chairs and tables available. These have great flexibility of use because they can be put away during the winter or brought into the house to augment existing furniture when extra guests are expected. They also have a more contemporary appearance: chairs often incorporate elegant styling effects created by the interlocking of the parallel seat and back slats.

Above: **In city courtyards, space is at a premium. Folding aluminium chairs are light and compact, and can be taken in and out in a trice. These two examples are smart enough to take to an open-air gala.**

Left: **The ubiquitous folding deckchair is practical and cheap. The addition of arms in this design makes sitting down and standing up much easier.**

If you are happy to have a table that is a permanent fixture, consider other natural materials. Slate and granite make magnificent tops that weather and age naturally; the surfaces can be either polished or hammered to a fine patina, revealing their subtle colour variations of greys, greens or reds. Although similar in appearance, marbles tend to break down too much and may also stain.

Stone tables are extremely heavy and impossible to move around, so if you are after something special, but a little more manageable, consider zinc. Just like for bar counters, it is used in sheet form and fixed smoothly over a wooden base. It is a very new look, smart, casual, and good for a contemporary terrace.

If these options are not to your taste, there are many other materials. For example, metal furniture has long been popular. It has a special kind of elegance, whether it be the fine, reeded, wrought ironwork of the Regency period or the cast-iron designs of Coalbrookdale, with foliage, fruit and flowers in sumptuous relief. Today, cast metal pieces are usually made of lighter aluminium.

Top left: **Intricate designs are a feature of cast iron. Fruiting vines decorate the arms and legs of this timber slatted bench, which is brought right up to date with a coat of soft grey-blue paint.**

Top right: **This curvaceous, wooden, arts-and-crafts furniture has taken on a lovely, silvery patina with age. It is subtly complemented by the antiqued wirework basket on the table.**

Above left: **A convenient pair of trees is not always available. This is a good example of an attractive, free-standing hammock. However, the cradle-like frame needs lots of space to work visually.**

Above: **In a tiny garden, every inch of space has to earn its keep. This brick and timber unit makes room for people as well as some fresh herbs.**

Opposite (top left): **Completely weatherproof and excellent mimics of natural cane, new woven plastics are taking over the garden furniture industry.**

Opposite (top right): **Enduring and weathered, this wooden bench doubles up as a workbench and display area.**

Opposite (bottom left): **A barbecue area beside a pool has been made from white in situ concrete.**

Opposite (bottom right): **Folding chairs are easy to move around.**

One of the most emulated metal chairs is the pretty French café design, utilizing curving lyre formations in the back with a woven slatted seat. It was developed from the bentwood furniture of the late 19th century. The other French classic from that period incorporates a circle of sprung metal segments in the seat and back, which incurve when sat upon; it is surprisingly comfortable.

Wirework furniture was also popular in Europe at that time and its popularity continued during the 20th century. Its beauty is its capacity to be curved and twisted into a multitude of shapes; it has a charming fragility, but is nevertheless strong. This versatile medium keeps enjoying revivals and examples can be found from traditional Gothic styles to 1950s funky.

However, it is in the realm of materials such as nylon and plastic that garden furniture can reveal its full potential. Often combined with aluminium frames, these materials are strong but light, making the furniture easy to move about. They can be translucent or opaque in a kaleidoscope of boiled-sweet acids to tropical hues.

When it comes to colour, we should not forget the humble deckchair: it is cheap, comfortable and bang up to date when covered with striped canvas. Directors' chairs can be found in smart canvas, ranging from grey and cream checks to navy and white stripes. If you have some tired old chainstore versions, freshen them up with a paint job and some wild fabric.

Garden seats for sitting are much more comfortable with cushions, which also gives an opportunity to update the look. Fabrics in plain colours, stripes and checks look the smartest; florals seem to be in competition with the plants, and not very successfully at that.

Hammocks are a fun form of casual seating. Made from canvas or crocheted string, they are just the thing for lazy weekends with a good book. They look best slung between two trees, where the occupier can benefit from the leafy shade. You can buy cradles to support them, but the effect of this contraption is rather contrived. Better to save up for a swing seat with an integral canopy; they even come in queen size, so there is no need to fight for possession.

The rapid evolution in garden furniture design is closely following our changing lifestyles, our taste in clothes and even our eating habits. The pressure on available living space has driven the re-development of vast industrial buildings into glamorous apartments and penthouses, whose outside spaces demand a totally different approach from the traditional country garden. Slick looks and startling kindergarten colours are much in demand for these city terraces and roof gardens where owners seek an immediate expression of their own new thinking spirit and vitality.

These spaces provide not so much an escape from frantic daily life but rather an extension of it. This is an "artificial" garden space for instant effect and short term, good weather gratification. It reflects the latest smart restaurant and the avant garde art gallery, stimulating fast talk and amusement.

For the design purists, traditional materials are emerging in minimized reincarnations. Timber steaming methods enable streamlined, flowing forms while metals are pressed into tables and seating with smoothly sinuous lines. All these sensuous curves generate a

Above: **Massive planks of planed timber make a dramatic and unusual dining table.**

Below: **This erotically suggestive red plastic "love seat" demonstrates the sculptural possibilities of this versatile material.**

voluptuous sense of freedom and relaxation, encouraging long dreamy afternoons and evenings of good food and deep conversation.

Plastics and synthetics, once shunned as an outdoor material, introduce some of the most desirable designs now available. Welcomed for their lightness of weight, they pose no threat to roof gardens and balconies and are easy to move around and store. They introduce attractive textures that emulate impractical traditional materials such as rattan, string and canvas, while having properties tough enough to be left out in all weathers.

On the other hand, moulded designs can make a dramatic architectural statement introducing a piece of practical artwork into the garden. Injection-moulded plastics in bold and brilliant colours can introduce a startling, surreal element while complex resins can be made to emulate valuable minerals like bronze and copper.

One of the most unexpected materials to emerge in outdoor furniture design is concrete. New moulding techniques and a better understanding of composition, colouring and finishing have led some creative artists to develop completely original forms. Now, sinuously sensual seating, together with robust tables and planters, are introducing a new kind of "stone" to the modern garden.

Above: **The smooth curves of this modern teak furniture demonstrate a pared-down fluidity – a distant cry from bulky traditional hardwood furniture designs.**

Below: **A fabulous example of contemporary furniture design, this sensual bench combines a sinuous framework of moulded polished concrete with a curved timber seat.**

Left: **An unusual steel-clad dining table and curvaceous aluminium-framed chairs suit the cool, contemporary lines of this terrace. Metal furniture must be given a shaded position, however, to avoid burning.**

tree seat

The beauty of this three-part tree seat, which is made from oak, lies in its simple design and the ease with which it can be fitted around a tree. The loose construction of the seat means that it can also be moved indoors during poor weather. For this reason, it can be built from seasoned or unseasoned timber. Oak can resist weathering without treatment for 50 years or more.

Materials and Equipment

for the 6 seat supports:

thickness: at least 80mm (3in)

height: to suit slope of ground, but a minimum of 380mm (15in)

width: to match width of seat, but tapered inwards at the top by about 25mm (1in) on each side

for the 3 seats:

thickness: at least 80mm (3in)

length: 1200mm (48in), 1500mm (60in) and 1800mm (72in), depending on size of tree and the available wood

width: 230–450mm (9–18in), depending on the widths available

hardwood dowelling (sold in set lengths), 12.5mm (½in) in diameter

mallet and gouge

metal ruler

handsaw

electric drill and 13mm (½in) drill bit

sharp knife (to whittle pegs)

waterproof wood glue

drum sander attachment (coarse paper)

1

2

3

4

5

6

Preparation

Before starting work, check that the ground around the tree you have chosen is firm and well drained. If necessary, sink bricks or stones beneath the legs in order to provide additional support.

1 Using the mallet and gouge, chisel away the bark and sapwood from the wood around the edges of the legs.

2 Using the metal ruler and a pencil, mark the position of the legs on the underside of the seat. The first line should be about 90mm (4in) from the end. The distance between the two lines should match the width of the legs. Mark the edge of the wood to a depth of 25mm (1in).

3 Saw along the marked lines.

4 Create a 25mm (1in) deep slot at each end of the seat by chipping away the wood with the mallet and gouge.

5 Cut 12 pieces of dowelling to a length of just under 25mm (1in).

6 Drill two holes in the centre of the top of the legs, 150mm (6in) apart and 25mm (1in) deep, to hold the dowelling. Drill corresponding holes in the slots in the seat.

7 Glue the ends of the pieces of dowelling and tap in place in the holes on the underside of the seat.

8 Glue the other ends of the dowelling and slot the two legs in place. Hammer firmly into place, and wipe away any surplus glue. Level the seats into place.

9 Smooth the seat using the drum sander. Treat with wood preservative or linseed oil (optional).

7

8

9

Obtaining Timber

Before deciding on the type of wood to use, it is advisable to visit a specialist timber supplier who can provide advice on a range of different woods as well as on their suitability for this project. Choosing the type of wood raises the issue of weather-resistance, durability and appearance. Preservatives can sustain the life of almost any timber, although hardwoods, such as the oak, do not need to be treated with a preservative.

The combination of colours and the simple design of this mosaic table makes for a striking piece of furniture. The table can be used outdoors in good weather, as it has some weather resistance, but you will need to bring it inside during very rainy periods and for the winter because it is not completely weather-proof.

mosaic table

Materials and Equipment

5 copies of the template on page 248
tracing paper and 2B pencil
drawing pin and string
masking tape
marine plywood or exterior grade plywood, 13mm (½in) thick
PVA (white) glue
paint brush
glass mosaic tiles in off-white, light verdigris, dark verdigris, moss, gold-veined verdigris, gold-veined green
tile nippers
goggles
flexible knife
cement-based, water-resistant tile adhesive
cement-based, water-resistant grout
small bucket
tiler's spreader
sponge and soft cloth
rubber gloves

1 

2 

Preparation

Mark out the circumference of the table top, using a 600mm (24in) piece of string tied to a drawing pin at one end and a pencil at the other. Push the pin into the centre of the piece of plywood, then draw the circle, rather like a compass. Cut out using a jigsaw.

1 Enlarge the template, following the instructions on page 248. You will need five copies of this template. Cut out each template and stick together with masking tape to create the whole design. Using the pencil, trace the design on to the tracing paper. If the pencil markings are not strong enough, draw over them with a felt-tip pen.

2 Turn the tracing paper over so that the pencil lines are facing down. Place on top of the piece of plywood and rub over the lines of the design with the pencil.

3 Seal the board with diluted PVA (white) glue, making sure you seal the rim of the plywood as well.

4 Using the tile nippers, and wearing the goggles for safety reasons, cut the tiles into halves and thirds so that you have a variety of different widths. Make a small pile of each colour and save some whole tiles to nibble with the tile nippers into different shapes and sizes later.

5 Mix up the tile adhesive in a small bucket. Using a flexible knife, spread it over one area at a time, approximately 3mm (⅛in) deep. Select off-white, light verdigris, dark verdigris and moss-coloured mosaic pieces. Press them into the tile adhesive, leaving a tiny gap between each piece. Wipe away any adhesive spillages immediately.

3

4

5

6

7

8

6 Fill in the area inside the ring with the gold-veined verdigris and gold-veined green mosaic pieces. In order to achieve a neat finish in the centre of the design, nibble the tiles into wedge shapes.

7 In the same way, stick down the outside rim of the rounded petal using the light verdigris, dark verdigris and gold-veined verdigris mosaic pieces.

8 Fill in the rounded petals with the light verdigris, dark verdigris, gold-veined verdigris and gold-veined green pieces. Nibble them with the tile nippers so that they fit neatly within the rim of the petals.

9 Fill in the pointed petals with the gold-veined verdigris, gold-veined green, light verdigris and dark verdigris pieces.

9

10

11

12

10 Fill in the area between the flower design and the edge of the plywood with the off-white, light verdigree and moss pieces. Leave to dry for a day.

11 Wearing rubber gloves, mix the grout in the bucket. Push the grout into all the cracks between the mosaic pieces, using the tiler's spreader. Wipe the tabletop and edge with a damp sponge. Polish with a soft, dry cloth.

12 When the tabletop is dry, turn it over and spread the base evenly with the tile adhesive in order to seal it.

Right and far right: **Pretty and light, this table is an ideal spot for relaxing in the summer.**

containers

Above right: **A pedestal urn makes a good focal point for a parterre. Planting can be changed seasonally to alter the effect; this cascading froth of verbena and helichrysum makes an excellent horizontal balance to counteract the height of the display.**

Right: **This refined and understated sheet lead planter makes a dignified showcase for white flowers such as this charming lily-of-the-valley (*Convallaria majalis*).**

Below left: **Lead can be cast in a mould to form a complex design. The octagonal shape is a good foil for the low-clipped laurel.**

Below right: **A bunch of iron-work rods has been fashioned into a stylish support for an unusual cone-shaped pot.**

The container plays an important visual role in the garden, creating focal points among planting and emphasizing architectural features. It makes a statement of shape and form that is inseparable from the plants it supports. The container demands certain characteristics from the plant to complement it and the plant depends upon a certain style of container to set it off. The successful combination must then suit the garden setting. It is a balancing act of weight and volume with texture and style.

Containers look most effective when placed in an organized layout. They can be grouped together in a collection of varying heights and styles, lined out formally in a row of identical pots and plants, placed in pairs to frame an opening or positioned singly to balance another feature.

A "container" is any type of vessel that may be directly planted, or an outer jardinière to enclose one or more pots. There is barely a limit to the type of

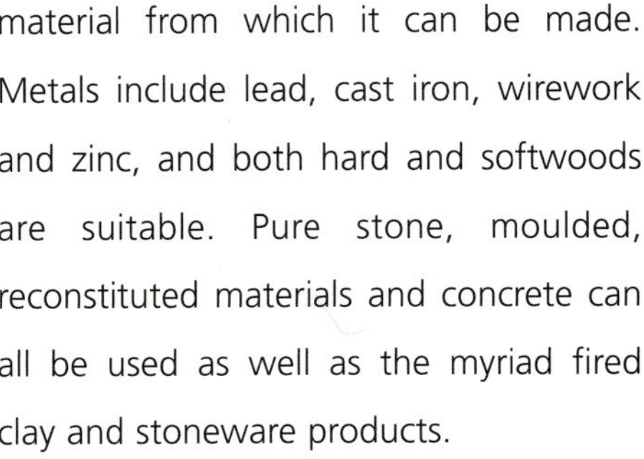

material from which it can be made. Metals include lead, cast iron, wirework and zinc, and both hard and softwoods are suitable. Pure stone, moulded, reconstituted materials and concrete can all be used as well as the myriad fired clay and stoneware products.

The classic garden container we all recognize is the terracotta pot. These pots are made all over the world in shapes that include simple cylinders, Ali Baba urns and elaborate hand-made vases. The colour and texture differ, according to the source of the clay and the temperature at which it is fired: 1200°C (2200°F) is the

minimum for any pot claiming to be frost-proof. If you live in an area that experiences freezing temperatures, do check that pots will withstand them. Colours range from pale creamy tones, through mellow umbers to rich brick reds.

The particularly special quality of terracotta, apart from a most sympathetic appearance, is its ability to breathe. Water and air can pass through the entire surface, so that soil dries evenly, not shrinking away from the sides. Terracotta also tends to keep roots cool, and the overall result is that plants have a relatively stress-free existence, allowing them to grow better.

Impruneta in Tuscany is the source of what is widely considered to be the Rolls-Royce of clays. The colour is normally deep umber to red, it has a very fine texture that minimizes water absorption (the main cause of frost damage), and it is exceedingly strong. These qualities, reinforced by superb traditional craftsmanship and beautiful design, result in containers of classical beauty that will last a lifetime. They do, however, have a price tag to match, although many would consider them a justified investment.

The weight of these pots requires them to be hand moulded rather than thrown, and before being fired they may have a surface decoration applied. These range from a simple rim and border to elaborate designs including garlands of fruits, such as the famous "lemon pots", which can be large enough to contain a 3m (10ft) tree. In England, one pottery specializes in a similar manufacturing

Left: **The versatility of zinc is demonstrated in this coolly chic container. The tall, tapering form is contrasted by planting with a tightly clipped box ball.**

Below left: **This vase is a classic form suitable for placing on the ground or on a pedestal. Found in terracotta, carved stone and concrete, this vase is made from weathered, reconstructed stone.**

Above: **The combination of container and plant is a matter for great care. The spiky brown stems of this bamboo, together with a green glass mulch, perfectly match the patina and shape of the narrow stoneware pot.**

Left: **A carved terracotta urn displays lions supporting a pair of pensive cherubs.**

process, using a secret recipe for white Coadestone clay, an extremely precious commodity. This has many of the properties of Impruneta clay, but is even smoother, resulting in creamy coloured containers of incredible beauty.

At the other end of the scale can be found simple long toms, beloved of Victorian gardeners. This rimless, tall and narrow shape is finding much favour now for its simplicity and style. A kitchen garden would not be complete without some traditional pots, and rhubarb forcers make great decorations.

It should be noted that there is a world of difference between a hand-made and a machine-made pot. Hand moulding is described above, but the method of production with which we are more familiar is throwing by hand on a wheel. This method results in very lively pots that can be drawn up tall and narrow or squashed flat and wide. Although the exterior would be finished smooth, the inside shows the rings created as the pot evolves. If you look closely, you may also see the potter's finger marks. In contrast, machine-pressed pots tend to have a rather dead quality, shiny surface and uniform shape.

Terracotta, especially from the Mediterranean, is often glazed in deep green, amber or marine blue. These colours look especially beautiful in a sunny climate. Pots seen glazed in more brilliant shades are usually made from stoneware, which is a harder and denser material. Although lacking the natural porosity of terracotta, stoneware nevertheless possesses special qualities of its own, and large vessels made from it are highly prized in the Far East. It can carry complex glazes, pale green celadon being one of the most famous; the deeper greens and blues are beautiful too. In Japan, these pots are often fired in wood-fuelled kilns to create special effects in the glaze, particularly resulting in dramatic browns and blacks. In northern Europe, salt is often thrown into the kiln, producing a silvery brown effect on the surface of the pot.

These weighty stoneware containers lend an Asian influence to the garden and are easily able to carry expressive plants with architectural foliage. Bamboo, phormium, yucca, aralia and palms all make good subjects. Low bowls and curving jar shapes make stunning water features that reflect light in their glaze.

When an imposing kind of formality is required in the garden, the Versailles tub must come top of the list. Its cubic form and emphatic weight make it most appropriate for formal woody shrubs and small trees, which reflect its classical style and underline its mass. The sight of massed ranks of the original planters in the Orangery at Versailles is overwhelming; literally hundreds of pale grey-green boxes, in sizes from 50cm to 1.5m (20in to 5ft) tall, containing mature citrus, bay, dwarf pomegranates, conifers and palm trees, are taken in and out between summer and winter. These were designed with removable side panels to facilitate root pruning and soil conditioning, and it is occasionally possible to find new versions of these. Variations of this classic shape, more normally seen in sizes around 50–80cm (20–31in), are perfect for framing a formal entrance door; Paris and London abound with them, usually planted with bay trees or box balls. This is definitely not the container for frothy summer bedding.

Tall, narrow planters in round or square shapes are fast coming into vogue, their cool, understated lines being well suited to chic, contemporary living. Some very elegant examples are made from zinc, which reinforces their cool styling. For settings where this look would be too metropolitan, they can also be sourced in glazed stoneware, terracotta and wood.

To work well visually, tall planters must be planted sympathetically. Shrubs such as box (*Buxus*) in ball shapes, and rosette-forming architecturals like *Sempervivum*, give the impression of a low cushion, which artfully balances the tall form beneath. It is advisable to avoid oversized or flowing specimens that run the risk of being top-heavy. Note that these tall planters should be positioned out of the wind because their only drawback is their small base in relation to height.

Roof terraces present special problems for the container gardener, not least those of sun and drying winds, and the major consideration of weight. Containers fitted with automatic irrigation systems are crucial to avoid the necessity of watering continuously by hand, and wide-bodied shapes will help with stability from winds. In order to reduce unnecessary weight, planters made from plastics and glass fibre (reinforced plastic) are very useful options. Some excellent designs exist, although unfortunately they will never achieve the weathered patina of natural materials.

Left: **Roof terraces present special problems of weight and space. Zinc, a relatively light metal, has been fashioned into bold rectangles, large enough to support the production of vegetables.**

Top left: **The gently rusting patina of this cast-iron vase subtly reinforces the seeding grasses surrounding it.**

Top centre: **Rusty chain has been used very imaginatively here to create a textured beachside planter. The grass and pebbles perfect the design.**

Top right: **The beauty and endurance of high-quality terracotta is embodied in this old Italian urn.**

Right: **Glazed clay pots integrated within the planting bring reflective qualities to the garden.**

Below left: **Old terracotta oil jars make excellent focal points among naturalistic planting.**

Below right: **The light weight of these impressive square zinc planters makes them perfectly suited for use on a roof terrace.**

Above: **Square shapes are notoriously difficult to make successfully, and these handmade pots take weeks to finish. The elegantly tall, contemporary containers are carefully balanced with a planting of low, clipped topiary.**

Left: **This row of hand-thrown, tall clay urns are raised on a tile-clad plinth to make a striking statement without any need for plants.**

Elegant terracotta pots can be transformed with a selection of carefully chosen paint colours. Painting pots means you can introduce a splash of colour quite easily to any corner of the garden. An arrangement of three pots in different sizes is guaranteed to make a statement, particularly if they are all planted in the same way. The colours used to decorate these pots are cool and sophisticated.

painted pots

Materials and Equipment

3 clean, dry terracotta pots in decreasing sizes
paint tester pots in grey-green, sage green, pale lemon, orange and French blue
paint brushes in a variety of widths
exterior-grade varnish

1

2

3

4

1 Paint the pot on both the inside and the outside with the base colour – in this case grey-green, but you can obviously design your own colour scheme. Apply a second coat as soon as the pot is dry.

2 Boldly paint stripes in sage green down the pot with a fairly wide brush, about 25mm (1in) wide. The effect will be more successful if you are as relaxed as possible.

5

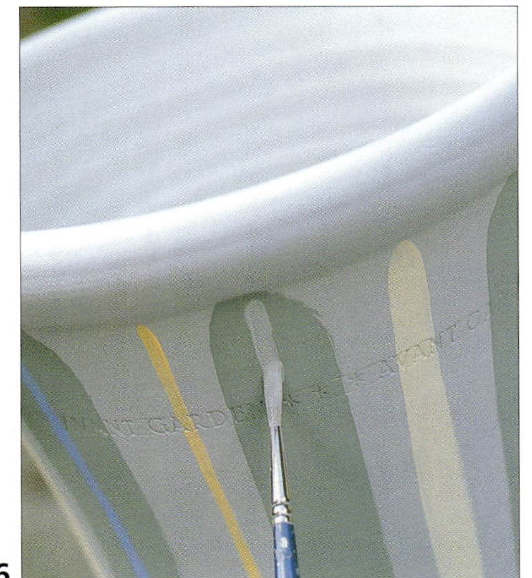

6

7

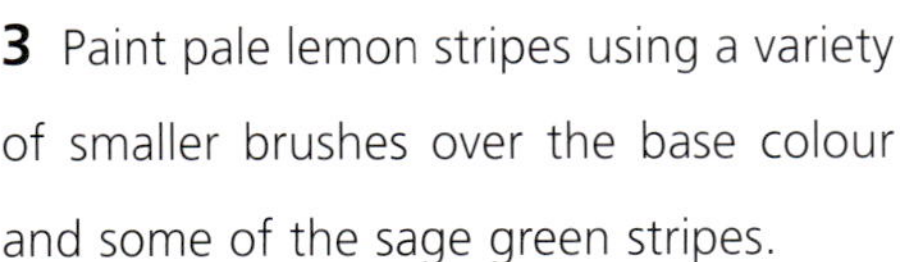

3 Paint pale lemon stripes using a variety of smaller brushes over the base colour and some of the sage green stripes.

4 Add the orange stripes.

5 Add the blue stripes.

6 Add stripes in the base colour on top of the remaining sage-green stripes. Repeat with the other pots. Keep standing back to check on the results of your labours.

7 Varnish the pots inside and out.

Above: **The pots look effective planted with the same plant, in this case a delicate bamboo with striped leaves. The layer of cobbles at the base of the pots adds a chic finishing touch.**

metal-trimmed planter

The lead strapwork of this timber-framed planter gives it a substantial, medieval look. The lead strips soon patinate to a lovely, whitish grey which gives the container an instant air of antiquity. The lead discolours with the effect of rain, but a white patina can be induced straightaway with the application of clear malt vinegar.

Materials and Equipment for a planter measuring 500 x 500 x 600mm (20 x 20 x 24in):

4 side posts, 50 x 50 x 600mm (2 x 2 x 24in)

8 side panels, 25 x 150 x 450mm (1 x 6 x 18in)

8 side panels, 25 x 150 x 500mm (1 x 6 x 20in)

4 base supports, 25 x 50 x 350mm (1 x 2 x 14in)

3 planks for base of planter, 25 x 150 x 445mm (1 x 6 x 17½in)

76 x 50mm (2in) screws

electric drill with a 5mm (¼in) drill bit

1 litre/1¾ pints/4 cups grey umber sadolin

lead strips (all 18mm/¾in thick):

4 side corner strips, 620 x 57mm (25 x 2¼in)

4 top edge strips, 510 x 65mm (20⅛ x 2½in)

12 horizontal side strips, 490 x 28mm (19¼ x 1⅛in)

8 vertical side strips, 610 x 28mm (24 x 1⅛in)

20 nails

80 galvanized metal pins

1

2

3

Preparation

If you are not confident of your wood-working skills, then simply purchase a wooden planter and apply the metal trimming, adjusting the measurements as appropriate.

1 Screw four of the side panels to two of the side posts, leaving 45mm (1¾in) at the bottom of the posts. Repeat for the opposite side of the planter, using the other two side posts and the remaining four 450mm (18in) side panels.

2 Turn over the panels and screw two of the base supports into position, using three screws for each support. The base supports should be flush with the bottom side panels.

3 Screw the four 500mm (20in) panels to each side.

4 Screw in the remaining base supports to the remaining sides, using three screws which are slightly staggered.

5 Using a saw, cut 50mm (2in) squares in the outer corners of two of the base planks. These will then slot over the corner posts and form the bottom of the planter.

6 Drill five evenly spaced drainage holes in the base planks, using the 5mm (¼in) drill bit, then slot the three base planks into position at the bottom of the planter.

7 Paint the planter, inside and out, with grey umber sadolin. Allow to dry. Apply another coat for a deeper stain.

8 Cut out all the lengths of lead strip, using a metal rule and a knife.

9 Place the 57mm (2¼in) wide lead strips into a vice as shown, and bend the strips down the centre so that they will fit round the four corners of the planter. In the same way, bend the top edge strips, but ensure that the split allows for 37mm (1⅜in) across the top and 28mm (1⅛in) down the side.

10 Lay out all the lead strips in position for one side. Position the horizontal strips first, laying them over the joins between the panels. Next, position the vertical strips, ensuring that they are evenly spaced – in this case, they are 125mm (4¾in) apart. Trim the strips down at this stage to ensure you achieve a neat finish.

11 Place the side corner strips and the top edge strips in position, starting with the corner strips.

12 Temporarily nail all the lead strips in place where they intersect, using a hammer and nails.

13

13 Replace each of the temporary nails with a galvanized metal pin.

14 Repeat the process of positioning and pinning the lead strips as well as adding the galvanized metal pins to the remaining three sides of the planter. Ensure that the vertical and horizontal strips are inserted under the corner and top edge strips.

15 Where the ends of the top edge strips overlap, cut into a 45-degree mitred corner as shown.

16 Using a wooden block, "dress" down or bend the edges of the top strips to form a neat edge at the top of the planter.

14

15

16

statues

The garden offers a uniquely sensitive and sympathetic setting for sculpture. It can provide a naturalistic landscape from which a sculpture suddenly emerges, surprising the visitor with its unexpected appearance, or a more formal situation where the sculpture makes a statement that can be seen from a distance.

The word statue implies for most of us an imposing figure presiding over an important square or piazza. It is certainly figurative, usually representing human form and at least life-sized, such as Michelangelo's David in Florence. Classical gardens around the world have always placed statuary in key locations to emphasize the architectural plan of the landscape; they might be representations of soldiers and statesmen, mythological gods or characters from children's stories. They might stand alone or be part of a fountain.

On a domestic scale, a statue may have to be content with being somewhat less than life-sized. The selection of a piece of sculpture is entirely subjective, and it cannot be overlooked that price must inevitably play a part in the decision. The degree of involvement by the maker and the cost of materials will have a huge influence on the cost of production; whatever budget you are working to, choose first for its craftsmanship, beauty and integrity. It may be far better to acquire a small bronze from an artist, to be set thoughtfully in a special position, than to give in to a large misrepresentation of Venus, cast in concrete, from the garden centre.

Right: **A treasured statue should be displayed with pride, as is the case in this alcove.**

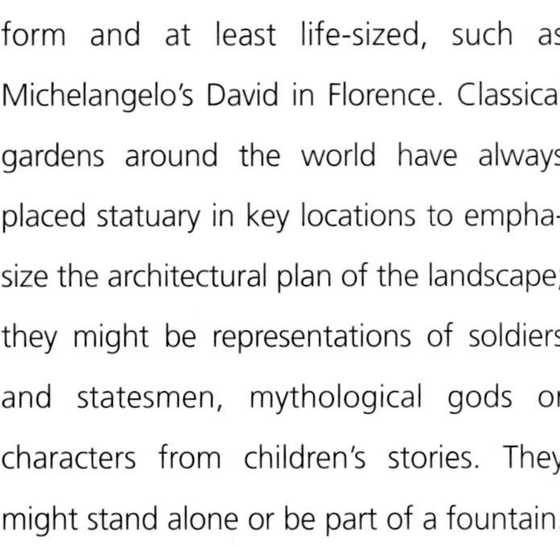

Above: **Terracotta is a pleasingly soft medium for a woman poised romantically among an underplanting of white roses.**

Left: **Quite small figures such as this patient angel take on a much more significant stature when placed on a plinth.**

Many makers of statuary advertise in the better gardening magazines; ask for brochures and visit them where possible to find the quality you want. Auction houses and specialist dealers are the best sources of antiques; with prices now reaching astronomical heights, it is essential to know the provenance and to be sure of the quality. Look out, too, for country-house sales and architectural reclamation centres where less prestigious items may be found among the serious treasures.

Left: **Dark green ivy provides a perfect backdrop for this refined carving of purest white marble.**

Below left: **A small stone figure set upon a tall column provides a sense of scale and emphasizes the change of level created by this flight of steps.**

Basically, a statue may be made of metal or stone. The former will usually be cast in bronze, a beautiful but costly option, gradually acquiring a warmly weathered patina and improving in appearance over time. Lead is an alternative option with a cooler appearance; cast iron is also used, but less frequently. Cheaper representations can be found made from resin combined with mineral aggregates; quality varies, so consider the finish carefully. As there will be no further weathering, it should look and feel as natural as possible when purchased, to guarantee enduring success in the outside.

Stone may be hand carved, although, because of quarrying and handling costs, this option is only really viable for smallish pieces. More likely, it will be cast in a combination of crushed stone and cement, or just concrete. This is the area in which most "off-the-shelf" work can be found; quality and style vary, but again, look for integrity of design and finish. Coloured tints and induced weathering are often incorporated to make pieces look aged.

Above: **A wall niche is an excellent feature of classical architecture in which to display a figure.**

Left: **A carved stone bust, elongated into a pillar, makes an excellent form to articulate the design of clipped topiary hedges.**

animal sculpture

Above left: **Cats are always popular sculptures and this cast bronze beauty is no exception.**

Above centre: **These bronze storks look as though they have just landed in the shallow pond.**

Above right: **A pair of hares, cast in resin, gambol playfully in the undergrowth.**

Right: **A lifelike pair of swans prepares to take off from a waterlily-covered lake.**

Opposite (left): **The strange appearance of the guinea fowl is captured beautifully in this group of sculpted forms.**

Opposite (centre): **A wise, old owl, cast in resin, peers imperiously from his hideaway.**

Opposite (right): **Carved stonework is a good medium with which to represent classical creatures such as this lion and ram.**

Perhaps the most popular sculptures in the garden are animals. They are our friends and helpers, setting fine examples of courage and integrity. We may have a favourite domestic pet or be interested in a particular wild breed and wish to represent its quirky characteristics or fine breeding. Childhood memories are very important, too, and it is especially comforting to be able to commemorate an old pal who gave us so much loyal support in our early adventures.

For a city dweller, access to wildlife is very often limited, so it would be refreshing to introduce some. The sight of a gaggle of geese on the lawn would create a welcome illusion of space and freedom. Transported from the country-side, a lone sheep, grazing in the moonlight, might introduce an air of surrealism, while a flock of pecking hens brings the cosiness of the farmyard close to home.

There is plenty of opportunity with animal sculpture to be amusing and light-hearted without being over-cute:

the animals may be caught in silly poses or be constructed from informal materials. There is a current vogue for making shapes from coarse wire mesh, which is built up in layers to achieve the final form. The finished result, say a life-sized goose or a sheep, is

often dipped in zinc to galvanize it or even sprayed with red oxide. Wire is an extremely versatile medium, and most effective visually; it is practical, too, because it is heavy enough to be stable while still remaining relatively easy to handle.

Hollow wirework forms make ideal "living animals" when covered over in evergreen ivy (*Hedera*). These exist in a variety of shapes, including peacocks, swans and alligators; some hand-made pieces are even handsome enough to stand alone unplanted, as sculptures in their own right. It is even possible to acquire a life-sized, moss-filled deer, installed with an irrigation sprinkler ready to water the lawn.

Recycling comes into its own in all types of sculpture. An exciting collection of creatures ranging in scope from ostriches to tropical fish is being produced in Africa from that enduring standby, used oil drums. Exotic plumage stands out in dramatic steel shards while clawed feet dance and tail fins flash, all finished in burnished bronze hues.

Amphibians and fish are the perfect companions for a water installation. Choose from verdigris bronze frogs on lily pads, terracotta carp ejecting spouts of water or introduce a haze of metalwork mayflies darting from fine wires.

If you seek to deter predators from precious fish stocks, a tall crane cast in bronze might have the required effect, especially if you move it around from time to time to confuse the optimistic fishermen. Conversely, to attract migrating wildfowl, some decoy ducks floating on a large pond may encourage rare visitors from far distant places to drop in for a pondweed snack. If your pond is to their liking, they may decide to spend their vacation with you and even build a nest.

The transitory movements of wildlife are easily immortalized in sculptural form. A bowl where birds drink and bathe can provide a permanent rest-stop for a stone robin or sparrow; a row of starlings might take up residence on a wall, or doves spend their days among the roof tiles. Half hidden in a flowerbed, stone hedgehogs can lurk, waiting patiently for worms, and, by the lawn, an optimistic bronze blackbird might contemplate an oversized brass snail, in reality a cunningly disguised sprinkler.

Working with willow is a traditional craft and, although it can be difficult to master at first, making something from a natural material is really satisfying. This pig is made from a mixture of hazel and willow, both of which can be found in woodland. However, you may need to contact a wildlife trust to find the material you need.

willow and hazel pig

1

2

Materials and Equipment

- pieces of wood to make the pig frame, about 60mm (2½in) thick
- 1–2 bundles of willow, depending on how fat the pig is to be
- 4 hazel sticks, approximately 500mm (20in) in diameter
- firm wire, 5mm (¼in) in diameter
- 8 nails, 80–90mm (3–3½in) long
- claw hammer
- electric jigsaw (optional)
- saw
- roll of chicken wire
- pair of gloves
- wire cutters or tin snips
- pair of pliers
- linseed oil (optional)
- white spirit/turpentine (optional)

Preparation

Although the stripped willow, graded in different colours, that is used by basket makers is readily available, "rough" willow is used to make the pig. This means that the bark is left on the willow. A bundle or "bolt" of rough willow contains pieces of willow in different lengths and thicknesses. However, if you have to buy graded willow, then ensure that you ask for unstripped black maul which should be no thicker than a pencil and about 1500mm (60in) in length. You will need about two bundles of willow in order to make the pig. The pig's legs are made from hazel, and a bundle of hazel always contains 25 sticks.

1 Make the frame for the pig's body using the template provided on page 249.

2 Nail the four legs on to the frame as shown. You will have to get the leg slots cut out by a carpenter unless you can do it yourself with a jigsaw. Try to angle one of the legs to create a sense of movement and to make the final pig look as natural as possible. Saw off pieces of the leg if necessary to ensure that the pig will stand level.

3 Trim off a small amount from the bottom of each leg to make the trotters.

4 Cut out a rectangular piece from the chicken wire. It should be approximately 1200mm (48in) long, but the width will depend on how fat you would like the finished pig to be.

5 Turn the frame upside down and position it on top of the chicken wire so that the back of the pig is approximately 300mm (12in) from the bottom of the netting. You will need more netting above the top of the frame to form the pig's head. Cut small slits at the legs and bend the chicken wire around the legs.

3

4

5

6

7

8

6 Using a pair of pliers, cut and join the chicken wire down the stomach of the pig.

7 Shape the nose with your hands until you are happy with the effect. Leave a fairly large gap at the throat of the pig, so that you will be able to fill the head.

8 Stuff the nose first with willow wands and continue filling until you reach the pig's back. Continue to add layers of willow, weaving through the netting and building up the shape of the pig. Keep standing back and viewing from all sides to check that you are happy with the overall effect.

9

10

11

9 Bend and weave pieces of willow in circles around the legs and the muzzle.

10 Decide on the position of the ears. Push the firm wire into place and bend into loops to form the ears. Stand back to check the effect because unnatural ears create an unnatural-looking pig. Start weaving the willow around the wire to build up the ears.

11 Cut out a circular piece of chicken wire to form the rear of the pig. Attach the piece of chicken wire to the pig's rear, in the same way as you joined the stomach. Weave and thread more willow through and around the rear of the pig until no more netting can be seen. Attach the tail. This is the thin piece of willow that is usually used to tie the bundles.

12

12 Check all round the pig for bald spots and add more pieces of willow to fill in and create a neat top layer. The pig is not completely weather-resistant and will need to be sheltered in poor weather and during the winter. However, it can be treated with a mixture of boiled linseed oil and white spirit (turpentine) at a ratio of 50:50 to improve its durability. Before applying the mixture, ensure that the pig is thoroughly dry, otherwise the moisture will be sealed in, rather than kept out.

Above: **The pig makes an amusing ornament for the garden and one which both children and adults love.**

abstract wood and stone

All pictures: **Abstract forms look especially effective when set within a garden or woodland. Two of these pieces of sculpture have been hand carved by an artist, using stones or forest timbers, while the other two have been created from carefully chosen finds.**

Above right: **'Pictish Spiral Bench' in green oak by Nigel Ross.**

Right: **'Small Mound of Stones' by Ivan Hicks.**

The appreciation of art is a subjective matter, each of us having our own ideas of beauty and form. Like any form of visual art, sculpture need not be figurative and representational, but can be subtly suggestive or totally abstract. In fact, the natural surroundings of a garden make an exceptionally appropriate setting for such contemplative work.

In the 20th century, we came to understand a different kind of vision, where human and animal structure was pared down to reveal fundamental elements of form and emotion. In a world documented by photography and film, we no longer needed representational evidence of existence, but sought to expose inner feelings, idealism and spiritual beliefs. The work of Henry Moore and Barbara Hepworth forged an artistic revolution in sculptural expression. Moore's monumental carvings of stone and marble exhibit both power and sensitivity, while Hepworth's curving forms proved inspirational, suggesting a route that many artists have since followed.

It is interesting to reflect that, following this emotional subjectivity, a new form of "super-realism" is emerging, in which everyday objects are reassembled to challenge our casual acceptance of familiar surroundings and world events.

One of life's greatest privileges is to own a uniquely created work of art. A carefully chosen and positioned piece of sculpture can entirely refocus a garden

Left: **'Old Balustrades' by Ivan Hicks.**

Below left: **'Trunks' made from carved and scorched oak trunks by Giles Kent.**

design, giving a lifetime of pleasure. Knowledge of the artist and the inspiration behind the piece adds immensely to our appreciation, while understanding how it is made and the influence the choice of materials plays on the appearance and visual weight also add to the experience. Vastly differing styles of work can be viewed at a growing number of garden sculpture galleries and parks. You can learn about the artists and, if you wish, commission a work. International events such as the Chelsea Flower Show in London are also an excellent way to meet artists and view new work.

Stone and wood both possess attractive tactile qualities and each lends itself excellently to hand carving. Stone and marble are physically heavy, cool and hard to work. Their provenance and composition determine whether they take on a smooth, gleaming sheen or a rougher, granular texture when refined and polished. Though heavy, wood can suggest less visual weight and the appearance and feel are warm and yielding. Its character is revealed in the internal structure of graining and knots, and it is relatively easy to work.

The inspiration to create a piece of sculpture often comes directly from the shape and texture of the subject to be worked. Giuseppe Penone pares back vast building construction timbers to reveal the emerging branches and tree from which they were originally hewn. Ancient root burrs can be fashioned into huge, intriguingly "marbled" balls. An artist will visit the quarry to select a particular seam or colour, or selecting a specific piece of timber.

Even without any experience of carving, you can create your own sculpture with "found" materials. A strangely contorted piece of driftwood or an ancient vine might be an interesting object in its own right, or a collection of pieces can be assembled in any way you find pleasing. They can be sawn, drilled and nailed, burnt or even painted, if that will help to create your desired result. Experiment with different textures and combinations, perhaps incorporating other materials such as rope or stone.

Take inspiration from the Japanese Zen gardens with a collection of stones piled up in the form of a tall cairn. Flattish pebbles of varying colour and size make an interesting "totem pole" when balanced on top of each other. Larger pieces of rock might be arranged into a druid offering that emulates Stonehenge. The only limit to the effects you can create is your imagination.

Benches and chairs set at strategic places in the garden provide good focal points and resting places, but need not be highly sophisticated in design. Bark-covered logs, willow, chestnut and hazel are traditional materials that can be woven or nailed together into quirky seats. These tend not to be very comfortable or durable, but they do make good talking points. Simpler seats and tables can be built from substantial rustic poles, and will last for years if constructed strongly.

Where something sturdier and more practical is required, an impressive table with benches built from slabs of green oak would make a strong statement. The most pleasing forms are often the simplest, created from thick, straight sections of timber on a square frame.

Benches make good decorative features in their own right; a single long wooden seat fashioned with flowing, sensuous curves would look magnificent, combining a dramatic sculptural statement with a congenial place to rest.

Ornamental furniture can be literally grown out of the ground to bring an organic effect to the garden. Living willow wands, planted in the early spring, can be woven into chairs or sheltering arbours, which will continue to sprout new green shoots each year. Free-form living willow sculptures are easy to create by twining long stems into shapes, and can be altered every season to take account of the growth pattern of the plants. Saplings of malleable trees such as birch, hazel, beech and hornbeam can be sculpted into arches or complicated forms, like love-knots, by bending and twining them as they grow.

Living topiary shapes bring natural ornamentation to the garden. Apart from classical forms like pyramids and balls, they are also trained into amusing birds and animals, sports equipment and even full sets of furniture. The medium is normally evergreen box and yew or miniature privet *Ligustrum jonandrum*, all of which are slow growing and expensive to plant.

However, a low budget and much simpler alternative can be achieved by twining small-leaved evergreen ivy around a wirework shape. You can make the frames yourself to your own design, or if this sounds daunting a variety of shapes can be sourced at flower shows and garden centres.

Above: **An old wooden ladder is turned into organic sculpture when decorated with a fringe of rusty garden nails.**

Below left: **This charming group of truly organic furniture is created by training *Ligustrum jonandrum* over wirework frames.**

Objects for use in garden decoration can come from any source. It is fun to collect wind-fallen branches on a woodland walk. The winter garden reveals all kinds of vine-like strands, such as willow, dogwood, bramble and ivy, all of which can be woven into baskets, screens or free-form shapes. Cones, nuts and seeds can be assembled into sculptures or strung into garlands. Gleanings from the seashore can include driftwood and rope, or if you are really lucky, remnants of net and pieces of an old boat. However, remember it is no longer permissible to remove stones or pebbles, and sometimes shells from public beaches.

Above left: **Massive blocks of solid oak make a bold sculptural statement and an innovative seating feature.**

Above right: **Everyday items, like these wooden clothes pegs, can be employed to create special visual effects.**

Right: **A huge vase woven from reeds cleverly mimics the form of the adjacent tree fern.**

metal

The garden makes an excellent sculpture gallery, as the planted surroundings and ever-changing play of light and shade provide the perfect setting for dramatic pieces of art, or eye-catching and amusing decorative features.

Metal sculpture in the garden over the last few centuries has been largely confined to figurative castings of bronze or lead. Although there seems little decline in the popularity of traditional subjects, artists are now creating modern pieces for the garden in a much more challenging, free and organic style.

Many sculptors and artists are now using steel to develop exciting forms that are expressly designed to be set within the garden landscape. Metals, with their ability to be cut, bent and welded, are a useful interpretative medium, and many unusual designs are appearing, often taking their inspiration directly from plants and trees. Sculptural fountains, often made from copper and featuring leaves and stems, are very popular, as are exciting lanterns and torches.

A current trend for rusty iron is often expressed in structures of untreated steel rods, which have a raw and understated charm that blends well with informal planting schemes. However, Cor-ten steel is in a completely different league. Specially manufactured to take on a fabulous patina of rich browns and golds as it weathers, it is a favourite with modern artists and sculptors, especially for slab-like and monumentally scaled projects.

Several outdoor galleries specialize in outstanding modern sculpture, while flower shows and local country events are excellent sources, attracting many up-and-coming sculptors and blacksmiths.

Left: **Cor-ten steel is beloved of sculptors for its massive strength and weathered texture and colouring. This dramatically slashed piece towers up to the sky.**

Above: **A copper gutter and rain chain provides a dynamic alternative to a drainpipe for directing water from the roof.**

Left: **Spiky planting and tall poles set with shiny metal balls, combined with a seating enclosure of rusting reinforcing mesh, merge into an amusingly chaotic courtyard feature that contrasts sharply with the cool façade of the house beyond.**

abstract metal

Until the late 19th century, the concept of using metal to form sculpture was confined to the casting of precious materials such as bronze or lead into representational statuary. Today, the immense and powerful works in welded steel by Naum Gabo and Richard Serra have made truly revolutionary inroads into our perception of contemporary sculpture.

Gabo was an early 20th century Russian pioneer of "Constructivism", which involved building up sculptures from simplified elemental parts. It was highly exciting for him to use the newly developed engineering techniques of riveting and welding to fix the weighty steel sheets together; famous work includes the huge but hauntingly beautiful "Constructed Head" series. Serra's recent work in the United States involves slabs of corten steel, 60cm (2ft) thick, 4m (13ft) high and up to 10m (30ft) in length. These are assembled to compose curving, narrowly parallel walls, reminiscent of a medieval souk, and seductively snaking circular enclosures of eerie and overpowering presence.

The use of steel for art makes sense when we consider the huge influence that this material has had on the construction of 20th-century buildings and transportation. There are many finishes and weights available for creative use. In a contemporary garden, polished stainless steel can be shown alone, in all its light-reflecting glory, or combined with water moving over its surface. Corten steel is intended to go rusty, but without staining or deterioration, making it a perfect material for combining with stone or concrete.

As we have seen, the word sculpture does not imply only an original work produced by a known artist. Sculpture need not be serious, and gardens can certainly benefit from a sense of mystery

All pictures: **Metals take on a different character depending on the way in which they are made. Cast pieces have a high degree of density, while a lighter effect can be achieved by hand-working the metal into fluid shapes, such as leaves, or through the creation of airy assemblages of fine wirework.**

and fun. Scrap yards contain a stunning array of pieces of rusting metal and mechanical parts, just waiting to be recreated into forms from your imagination. It is tremendously gratifying to recycle a piece of cast-off junk into a personal creation. Pieces can be incorporated into water features, hung from tree branches or intertwined with plants. They may stand alone as a massive statement or materialize from a border to create a clever surprise.

The visual quality of rusted steel is a bonus, looking completely at home among vegetation. Stainless steel can be polished to a high shine, or textured to various matt finishes; it does not rust so will always remain gleaming. Galvanized steel wire is flexible and can be fashioned into a multitude of forms or simply used to hold other components together.

Other metals have interesting qualities too. Copper, available in sheet or wire form, oxidizes to a green verdigris patina.

Opposite (left): **'Butterfly Gate' made from galvanized steel by Victoria Rance.**

Opposite (centre): **'Organic Form' in copper by Peter Clarke.**

Opposite (right): **'King and Queen' in bronze by Helen Sinclair.**

There are no rules to follow when creating and devising your own piece of sculpture: anything that excites you can be employed in your work of art. Reinforcing rods, balustrades, gears and washers, engine parts or fuel cans, service pipes and air-conditioning ducts are all potential components; there is no end to the possibilities when you think laterally. Ducting and large cans can also be utilized to make eccentric planters.

Non-rusting, shiny aluminium sheet is flexible and can be cut with snippers. Zinc and lead sheet can be folded and pinned over a wood base. Titanium is gently reflective, taking on hues that mirror the mood of the sky and light.

This is a dangerous field in which to operate, so prepare equipment and protective clothing in advance. If welding facilities are not available, drill, wire and bolt lighter-weight pieces together.

Above left: **Detail of 'Cosmic Tree' in copper by Peter Clarke.**

Above centre and above right: **'Euridice' in bronze by Helen Sinclair.**

Not all garden ornaments need be on a large scale or last for a long time. This metal mobile, which is made from discarded aluminium cans, is a case in point and could be used to adorn a tree or decorate a seating area. Being made of metal, it will inevitably rust, but it makes an enchanting ephemeral ornament for the summer.

metal mobile

Materials and Equipment

2 x 440ml (15½fl oz) or 500ml (17½fl oz) drink cans (both must be the same size)
medium-grade sandpaper
sharp nail
hammer
pair of gloves
sharp knife
pair of scissors or tin snips
screwdriver or pencil
16–18 clear glass stones or nuggets
masking tape
adhesive (suitable for metal and glass)
680mm (27in) thin wire
key ring or curtain ring

1

1 Using the sandpaper, gently rub the cans to remove the printed finish and reveal the bare aluminium. Take care not to crush the cans while doing this. You might like to leave the cans unopened at this stage in order to provide a firm surface on which to press.

2 With a sharp nail and hammer, punch two holes in one of the cans at the 12, 4 and 8 o'clock positions. Remove ring pull.

3 Pierce the side of the same can with a sharp knife and, using the tin snips or the pair of scissors, cut away the bottom of the can. Trim any jagged edges. Repeat for the top of the other can.

4 Starting at the open ends of the cans, cut 13–18mm (½–¾in) wide strips to the bottom. You should have 16–18 strips.

5 Roll each strip around a screwdriver or pencil to create the decorative scrolls.

6 Roll some of the strips up and some of them under.

2

3

4

5

6

7

8

7 Fix one of the glass stones to a strip of masking tape, then gently unroll a scroll until it will fit around the stone. Using the tape to hold the stone in place, place a few drops of adhesive around the edge of the stone. Remove the tape as soon as the stone has set (after 30 seconds or so).

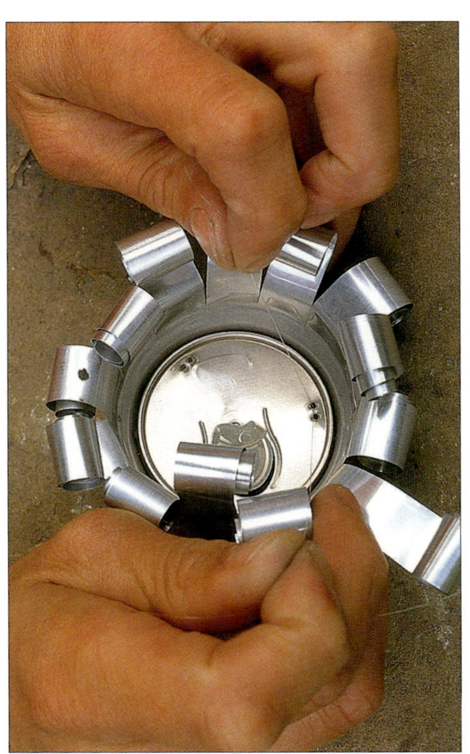
9

10

8 Continue to glue the glass stones in every other scroll.

9 Thread three pieces of wire, about 150mm (6in) long, through each pair of holes. Secure by twisting the ends.

10 Glue the two cans together, end to end. Once they are fixed, arrange the scrolls by gently bending the strips. Join the three pieces of wire at a central point above the mobile. Fix a final piece of wire at this point with which to hang the mobile. Twist this last piece of wire around a key ring or curtain ring. Make sure the mobile hangs straight.

living ornaments

We associate ornamental features in the garden with inanimate objects. However, plants offer a whole new dimension with which to create sculptural effects, utilizing shape and form, texture and colour. Shaping plants requires an understanding of growth patterns and seasonality, and reaps long-term rewards.

Topiary is the best-known form of plant sculpting. The species most commonly used are evergreens, including box (*Buxus*), yew (*Taxus baccata*) and bay (*Laurus nobilis*), but many other shrubs, such as camellia, rosemary and pyracantha, can give equally interesting results.

The main role of topiary is architectural, and the art has developed to include enclosures and objects. Clipped hedges are common in formal gardens: in avenues, as screening, backdrops for statues and boundaries for parterres. Heights vary from less than 1m (3ft) to perhaps 3–4m (10–13ft), depending on the scale of the site.

Yew is a favourite because it is a dense evergreen that grows to a good height and responds well to hard pruning, even down to nearly ground level. The only drawback is that it grows rather slowly. However, Lawson cypress (*Chamaecyparis lawsoniana*) is quick to establish and excellent if clipped regularly to keep it within bounds. Hornbeam (*Carpinus*) is also popular. It is tall and has thick summer foliage, but its deciduous habit means that it does not have such an enclosing spacial quality as evergreens.

Above: **A cast-resin mask is brought to life with a punk hairstyle of golden sedge.**

Above centre: **Topiary is the oldest form of living sculpture.**

Above right: **A pair of blue *Cedrus atlantica* f. *glauca* are twined together to form an archway. Any growth within the arch is removed to expose the form of the trunks and to encourage bushiness on the outside.**

Along the top of the hedge, shapes can be developed from the new season's growth. A castellated effect is possible, while figurative shapes such as birds and animals can tell a story or frame an entrance. The shape is entirely up to your imagination. Redundant hedges and overgrown bushes can be transformed into such bizarre creations as railway engines and ocean liners, rowing boats and helicopters. It is very fashionable at the moment to grow single shapes in a pot on a terrace; as topiary takes time to mature, these have the advantage that they can be taken with you if you move home.

Use hedging to develop the other forms of plant shaping, which start to become more akin to sculpture. For example, window holes cut into a hedge can open up an interesting vista beyond. A series of slots enable you to walk or look through to an adjacent area, while niches can serve to frame a sculpture or a seat.

Clipping is the way to contour dense shrubs, but other species can be trained differently. Left to their own devices, climbers tend to sprawl about quickly into a tangled mass of foliage and flower. By using a wirework frame such as a cone or a large ball, plants such as clematis, jasmine and passionflower can be formed into an elegant shape, revealing the individual blooms to perfection. Ivies can be trained in the same way to make instant evergreen obelisks planted in pots.

There are more avant-garde ways to train trees into shapes, utilizing the habit of bark to form itself over obstacles as the trunk grows in girth. Trees and shrubs can become real living sculptures. When young, all manner of trees can be twined into different shapes. You can create an archway or pergola by bending over two or more trees and tying them together where they meet. For extra panache, entwine the remaining growing points to form a ball or heart-shaped finial on top.

Architectural shapes such as obelisks, cones and spirals are useful devices for framing doorways and entrances and for use in formal parterres, where they can be used as vertical statements to emphasize the configuration of a design. In the Far East, the art of cloud topiary is popular for formal statements. This involves clipping back parts of the growth to reveal its structure while forming cloud-shaped blocks of foliage on the upper side of the bough.

Trees such as lime (*Tilia*) and hornbeam are often trained in a form known as pleaching. They are planted in line, 1–2m (3–6ft) apart, with the lower branches removed; then the upper branches are trained sideways along horizontal wires so that each tree ultimately intermingles with its neighbour. Formed into avenues, they allow a view between the clear trunks of the landscape on either side, while marking out the path with a block of foliage above.

Above left: **Conifers such as thuja and cupressus make dense, narrow forms. These two columns have been crossed over and tied together below the growing points, resulting in a strongly architectural arch.**

Above: **Individual plants, such as this *Agave americana*, make sculptural statements in their own right.**

Left: **The finished topiary clouds look absolutely spectacular against a blue, cloud-filled sky.**

Cloud topiary was originally created by Buddhist monks to reproduce, on a reduced scale, the asymmetrical appearance of mature, storm-ravaged pine trees. Drawing on the influences of both topiary and bonsai, cloud topiary transforms a bushy shrub into a miniature tree by using the inner framework of branches to support floating "clouds" of foliage. Cloud topiary looks striking in large decorative containers, but it is essential that you do not allow the soil to dry out.

cloud topiary

Materials and Equipment

a bushy shrub, about 60–120cm (2–4ft) high

coloured wool (yarn) or tape

pair of secateurs (hand pruners)

Suitable Plants

Box (*Buxus sempervirens*)

Japanese holly (*Ilex crenata*)

Japanese azalea (*Rhododendron*)

Orange bark myrtle (*Myrtus apiculata*)

Common myrtle (*Myrtus communis*)

Pine (*Pinus*)

Juniper (*Juniperus*)

Spruce (*Picea*)

Fir (*Abies*)

1

2

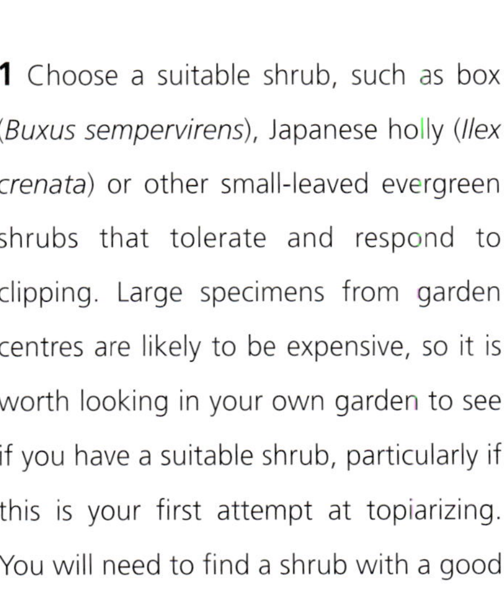

1 Choose a suitable shrub, such as box (*Buxus sempervirens*), Japanese holly (*Ilex crenata*) or other small-leaved evergreen shrubs that tolerate and respond to clipping. Large specimens from garden centres are likely to be expensive, so it is worth looking in your own garden to see if you have a suitable shrub, particularly if this is your first attempt at topiarizing. You will need to find a shrub with a good "bone" structure.

2 Open up the foliage to reveal the framework of branches. An ideal scenario is one or more main stems with strong side branches.

3 Decide which side branches to remove in order to thin out the structure. You should spend some time thinking through what you plan to do before starting to cut, and mark the ones to be retained with the coloured tape or wool (yarn). You will need to cut out approximately half the branches.

3

4

5

4 Cut out the unwanted branches, leaving behind more than you will actually need at this stage. Turn the plant around and stand back regularly to "see" the shape.

5 The individual heads of foliage can now be roughly clipped into pom-pom shapes. The clouds of foliage can eventually be developed into pom-poms or mushroom heads, although the latter is much more authentic. The individual clouds should vary in size and shape with a larger one at the top. There should also be adequate space between them.

6 Strip the leaves and smaller branches off the main branches that are to be retained.

6

7

7 Decide which branches or clouds are not required, but leave one or two within the framework.

8 Cut back the pom-poms quite hard to encourage dense, compact, new growth. As the piece develops, you might decide to remove individual clouds to prevent the plant from looking overcrowded. There should ideally be space between each cloud. Use wire or wooden splints to separate the branches if required.

8

Aftercare

Pruning should ideally be carried out in the spring after the threat of frosts has passed to prevent the new foliage from being burnt. Clip once or twice during the summer to maintain and improve the shape. The number of times you clip depends on the vigour of the plant. If the specimen is grown in a pot, it will need feeding as well as watering. Shrubs grown in pots are very vulnerable to drying out because they show no signs of damage until the worst has been done. Topiary is expensive and requires lots of care, so ensure that your specimen does not dry out.

lights

Right: **Candle lanterns make attractive and flexible garden lights.**

Top right: **A delicately formed, miniature, wrought-iron "candle tree" blends beautifully with the surrounding planting.**

Centre: **Low-voltage "fairy lights", wound around these metal frames, create a magical night-time effect in this vine tunnel. The addition of tiny spotlights at ground level accentuates the theme and helps to guide visitor through.**

Opposite (top): **Well-designed, stand-alone electric fittings can make a feature in their own right. This brass, mushroom-shaped downlighter marks and illuminates a flight of steps.**

Opposite (centre): **This magnificent, wrought-iron entrance gate is crowned by a splendid coach lamp in order to light the way at night.**

There is one service that you can provide to transform your garden at a stroke, and that is to install lighting. A lit garden becomes another room, an extension of the house instead of a black hole; this is a bonus in summer but a real boon in winter, especially for gardeners far from the equator. Many garden enthusiasts have to be content with seeing the garden only at night during the working week, so the benefits stand out immediately.

Light fittings are available in enormous variety and can be separated into the categories of security and display, up-lighting, flooding and highlighting. Up-lighters generally deliver the most sensitive effects, with subtlety being the key to success. Envisage the result you want, and try to achieve it with the smallest fittings available.

To guide the way along paths and to mark the edge of a pool, terrace or steps, small fixed up-lighters set into the paving blocks are subtle and attractive. They can

be used in conjunction with special effects such as glazed obelisks or wirework columns to create a formal entrance or mark a pathway. To illuminate a light-well, crushed windscreen glass spread over a broad transparent cover will hide the lamps and diffuse the light in a textural way, making it look like a pool.

Directional up-lighting works well to highlight a sculpture or to backlight a water feature; it can also make a soft

wash for the elevations of the property. Generally, trees and plants look best lit from underneath to reveal their shape and form. The appearance of a dramatically branching specimen tree illuminated at night is magnificent.

Pin-sized light beams make delightful fairy-tale effects. They can emerge in twinkling groups from hanging lanterns, be distributed like a mist through ground cover on tiny stalks, or fixed in strips to make a feature from the edges of steps.

Floodlights are easy and cheap but need to be used with care; avoid the football stadium syndrome at all costs. If you are concerned about intruders, install movement-sensitive trip switches that operate the lights only when triggered.

The perfect lighting scheme would be installed during the garden's construction, so that cabling is disguised and lamps positioned discreetly. If this is not possible, wall-mounted exterior lamps are the answer. They can be sourced in carriage-lamp style or in contemporary forms.

Ready-made sets of up-lighters that stake into the ground can be purchased from garden centres, but avoid those with lurid coloured lenses. When sited with care, the white lights are acceptable.

It must be stressed that electricity needs to be firmly and securely separated from water, wet soil and garden users. A qualified expert must make electricity connections to the main house, and any large installation is a job for professionals.

Candlelight is the gentlest and perhaps the best way to create ambience. Tea lights are cheap; set them in jam jars or hanging tin lanterns, line them up steps and along walls. Regular candles are best used in glass hurricane lamps to keep them from breezes. The nicest ones are hand blown, tall and set on high necks. However, all kinds of candelabra look romantic in the garden, and the running wax just adds to the baroque effect. Special garden candles have thick wicks that stay alight even in a storm; these create smoke and should never be used indoors. Candle or oil-burning torches to push into the ground are great for parties and big entrances.

Water is a fundamental element of life. Our bodies are almost completely composed of it, and all living things rely totally on water to exist. So, it should be no surprise that water has such a sublime effect on our spirits. When trickling or bubbling, water is soothing, while the energy and noise of a crashing cascade can be stimulating. This is an important quality to consider, as there is a world of difference between the relaxing effect of slow-moving water and the insistent noise of a dynamic installation.

water features

Right: **Light-filled droplets are one of the loveliest features of moving water. Rather oversized for bathing, a peacock looks on with disdain.**

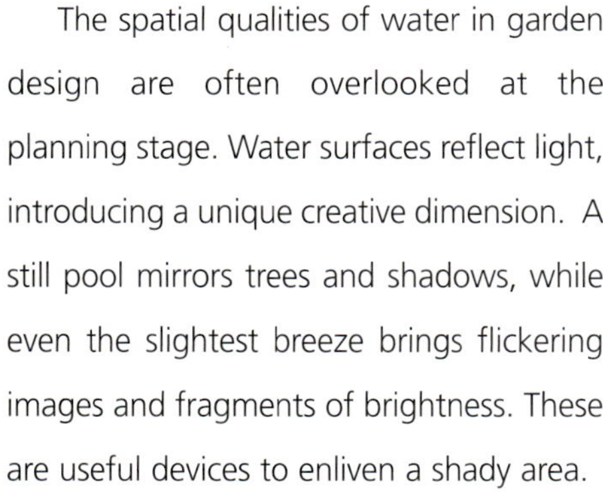

The spatial qualities of water in garden design are often overlooked at the planning stage. Water surfaces reflect light, introducing a unique creative dimension. A still pool mirrors trees and shadows, while even the slightest breeze brings flickering images and fragments of brightness. These are useful devices to enliven a shady area.

In areas of dense or busy planting, there is a danger of a kind of visual indigestion. Where there are a lot of competing architectural features, there can be so many distractions that the main point of focus is lost. Water, with its inherent vibrancy, creates a cool, visual gap with qualities very different from those of inert paving. In a controlled design, a rectangular pool could substitute for a gravel parterre, whereas in less formal surroundings, a simple pond would be appropriate. The physical and sensual qualities of water are the same, whether it is formally controlled in a restricted space or allowed to range freely over a large area. However, the resulting impression will be very different in these diverse situations.

Top: **This is a simple idea and looks so stunning. Thin copper pipes emerge, reed-like, from the pond to release fine jets of water through the dappled sunlight.**

Left: **This is a simple and effective idea that can easily be adapted to suit a wide variety of styles by changing the base receptacle and the style of the spout.**

It is probable that the majority of us have to be content with a small water feature in our garden, and consequently it is likely to be of a more formal nature. It is possible to buy ready-made pieces, but they have limited scope with results tending towards the banal. Small, self-contained units often look like superfluous bits of decoration. The reason is simply that, if water is to be successful, it needs to be treated as part of the landscaping design, built into the construction, not placed on the surface.

Left: **This cascade over a wall is designed to look as though it falls from a stream on a higher level. It has, in fact, been created with the help of a pump that recirculates the water from the reservoir below.**

Below left: **A small, carved gargoyle, set in a niche, releases a steady flow of water into a shallow stone stoup.**

Once you start to play with the idea of moving water, you begin to see more and more possibilities. One thing to remember is that, whatever the scale of the water project, the principle of the system remains the same. A holding situation at the lowest level is filled with water where the pump is situated; the pump circulates the water by pushing it up to the highest point, from where it will descend to the bottom again. An electricity supply, which should be installed professionally to meet exterior standards, is required, and thought should be given to hiding the pump and the cable.

Results are invariably more interesting if a special design is created using attractive elements. Even in its simplest incarnation, a hand-carved bowl will make a birdbath or an elegant dish in which to float flowers.

Architectural salvage yards are great sources for water troughs, carved bowls, pool edging, masks and fountain statuary. Landscape suppliers can provide rocks and stones, while specialist garden stores offer lead, terracotta and stone containers.

Above: **Wall fountains can be created in many different styles. This has been built to match the wall, using local flints, and, being in an area where there are a number of ecclesiastical buildings, it includes a relic from a derelict church.**

Left: **Water channels can be adapted to both classical and contemporary designs. This is part of a large system that was created by William Kent in the 18th century.**

Left: **It is always refreshing to see humorous touches in the garden; these welded steel crows disgorge water from their huge bills.**

Below left: **Mythological gods are perennial favourites for water gardens.**

Below centre: **The transparent and light-reflecting qualities of glass work well with water.**

Below right: **Carved granite balls combine excellently with the gentle trickle of water falling over them. These would work well in either a contemporary or Japanese design.**

Capitalize on water's gravitational urge to run down from a high level to a succession of collecting points below. Steps are an obvious example, and lend themselves to a contemporary garden, where water running down slabs of white limestone set off by borders of black slate could make a transition from a terrace to a pool below.

It is possible to adapt designs to suit any style simply by changing the components. For a woodland effect on a slope, "steps" can be composed of large rocks over which water can either crash dramatically or trickle gently. Instead of falling water, it can be induced into a shallow stream bedded with gleaming river pebbles or black slate fragments. Slate is a lovely stone to use with water because its green, grey and black tones complement water perfectly; it can even be used without water to present the image of a running stream.

The linear progression of a stream can be utilized to divide a garden into areas or to differentiate between levels. This idea

Right: **A small battalion of indignant carp defend their side of the stream from intruders.**

Below left: **This trio of columns of slate discs makes an effective visual statement, highlighted in the sunshine by water spilling down the sides.**

Below centre: **In this engaging sculpture, a tousle-haired water carrier deftly supports a shallow bowl above a leaden tank.**

Below right: **Brilliant blue and turquoise tiles give a Mediterranean feel to this tiny pool in a terracotta courtyard.**

works excellently in a formal situation when water fills narrow channels bordered by paving slabs to bring visual relief. If on a single level, it may be static but shallow level changes can be accommodated too. Bear in mind, though, that the resulting mini waterfalls would need to be controlled by a pump.

If you hanker for living art, give your creative energies full reign and make a dashing water sculpture. This could involve a series of vessels with water cascading from one vessel to the next. A central, free-standing, hollow steel tube could allow the water to pass upwards, releasing it from the top into collecting cups arranged down its length. If this type of water feature appeals to you, it is important to consider that some technical skill will be required to create it. Our project for a steel water feature on pages 246–247 will provide inspiration for a similar design and is a simple idea that can be adapted to your own garden.

steel water feature

This stylish, contemporary water feature is made from three stainless steel tubes. The water tumbles from slits in the tubes as well as over the top and down the sides of each one. Other materials, such as terracotta, plastic and copper, could also be used. The splashing sound can be "tuned" by adjusting the water pressure.

Materials and Equipment

plastic reservoir tank, about 600mm (24in) wide and 600mm (24in) deep
sand/geotextile fleece
polythene (plastic) pond liner
submersible water pump (maximum flow 3720 litres/819 gallons per hour)
25mm (1in) galvanized metal grille
fine plastic shade netting
plastic water pipe, 25mm (1in) in diameter
plastic water pipe, 13mm (½in) in diameter
3 x 13mm (½in) flow taps
5 x 25mm (1in) clips
three-way T-piece
3 x 100sq mm (1.5sq in) stainless steel tubes, 800mm (31in), 1000mm (39in) and 1200mm (48in) high
25mm (1in) to 13mm (½in)
shovel
hacksaw
screwdriver
wire cutters

1

2

Preparation

A steel fabricator should be able to supply you with some stainless steel tube. The cheapest option is to use standard-size pipes. Here, we used 100sq mm (1.5sq in) pipes in three cut lengths of 800mm (31in), 1000mm (39in) and 1200mm (48in), with a base plate and 13mm (½in) inlet pipe welded to each pipe. The pipes were bead-blasted to give a matt finish. To cut the slots into the pipes you can use a quality hacksaw. The ideal height for the slots is 50–100mm (2–4in) from the top of the pipes – any further from the top and the water will flow out too far.

1 Clear and level an area approximately 1800sq m (72sq in) to a depth of about 50mm (2in) with sloping sides. Within the cleared area, dig a hole approximately 600mm (24in) by 600mm (24in), or large enough to suit the size of reservoir. Ask a qualified electrician to dig a trench for the power supply, for which you will need an outdoor socket or waterproof junction box. Insert the container in the hole, making sure it is level and flush with the cleared area. Backfill with soil or sand if necessary.

2 Once the reservoir is level, line the cleared area and reservoir with geotextile fleece or sand. Using a sharp knife, cut a hole in the fleece above the reservoir.

3 Lay the pond liner over the fleece and the reservoir. Gradually add the water to the reservoir in order to pull the liner into place, remembering to fold the liner flat over the cleared area. Stand the stainless steel pipes on top of the liner next to the reservoir, in the desired configuration, making sure the pipes are vertical.

3

4

5

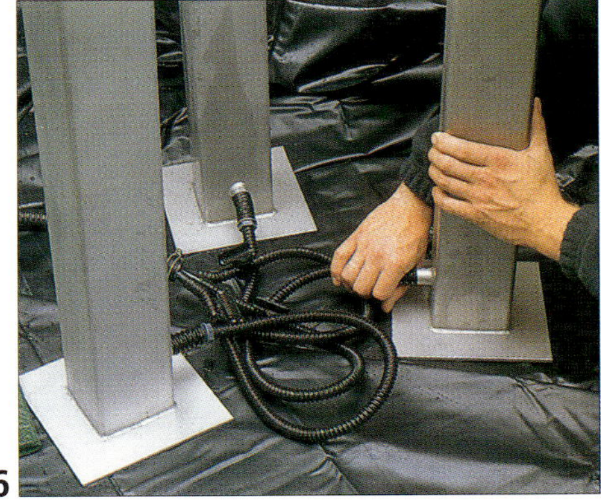
6

4 Place the pump in the reservoir and cover with the galvanized metal grille. Cut out a hole for the pipe to pass through.

5 To keep back finer particles, cover the metal grille with fine plastic shade netting.

6 Connect up the 25mm (1in) hose to the pump secured by a clip and connect the other end to the 25mm (1in) to 13mm (½in) three-way T-piece. Connect each of the outlet pipes to the 13mm (½in) hose and flow taps, which are then connected and secured with clips to the inlet pipes on each of the steel tubes. Cover over with cobbles, rocks and gravel. Turn on the power and adjust the flow of water as required.

Care and Maintenance

Evaporation will reduce the water supply, but the reservoir can be easily topped up by pouring water through the cobbles. There are a number of chemical products available for recirculating water features which keeps them free from algal growth.

Warning

Ask a qualified electrician to install all the outdoor sockets, switches and circuit breakers that are required for this feature.

Templates

To enlarge a templates trace the design and draw a grid of evenly spaced squares over your tracing. Draw a larger grid on another piece of paper and copy the outline square by square. Draw over the lines to make sure they are continuous. If you prefer, enlarge them on a photocopier.

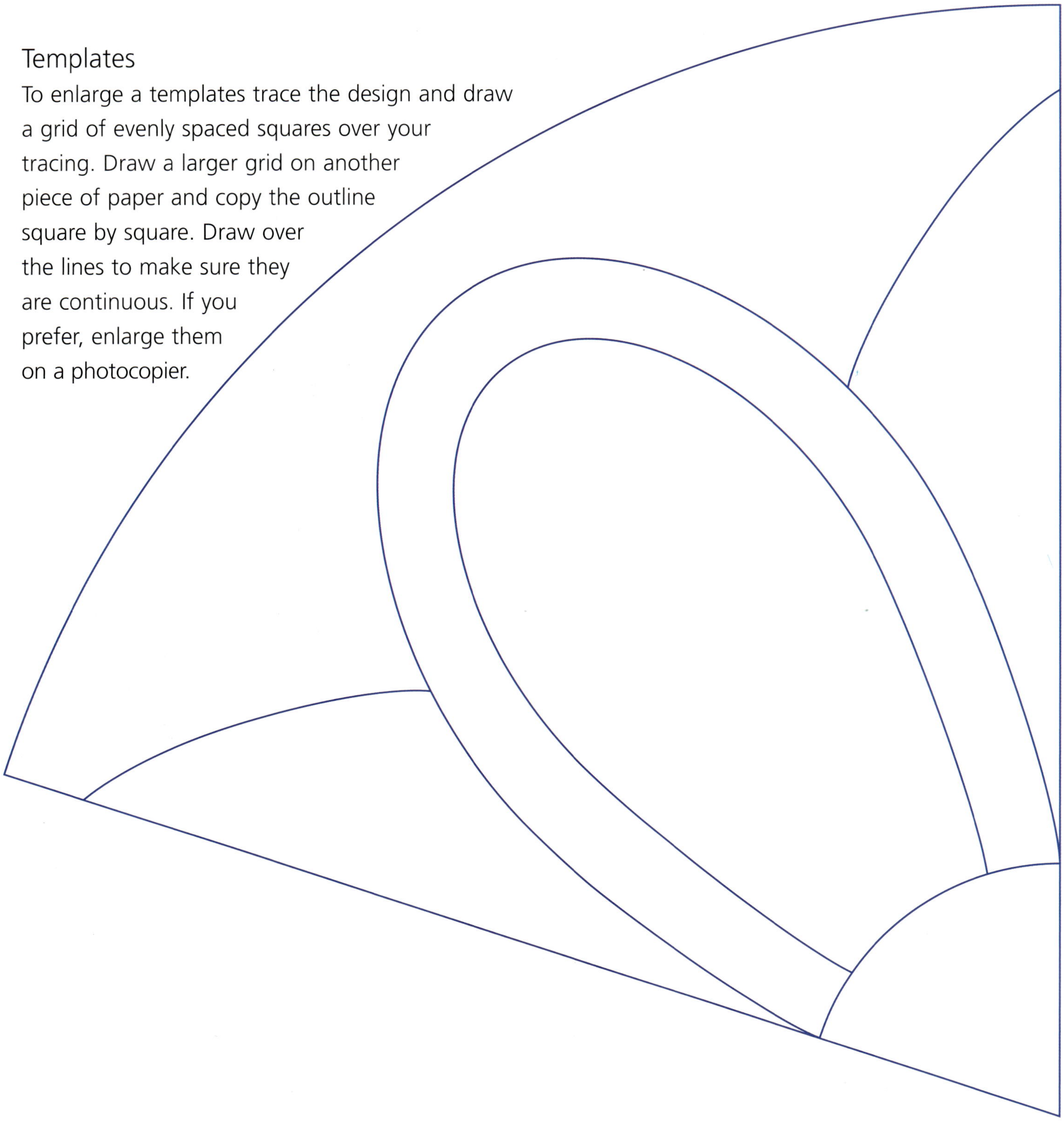

To make the Mosaic Table featured on pages 198–201, you will need to enlarge the template above by 146%. This template represents a one-fifth segment of the whole mosaic design, so you will need to enlarge five templates and tape them together.

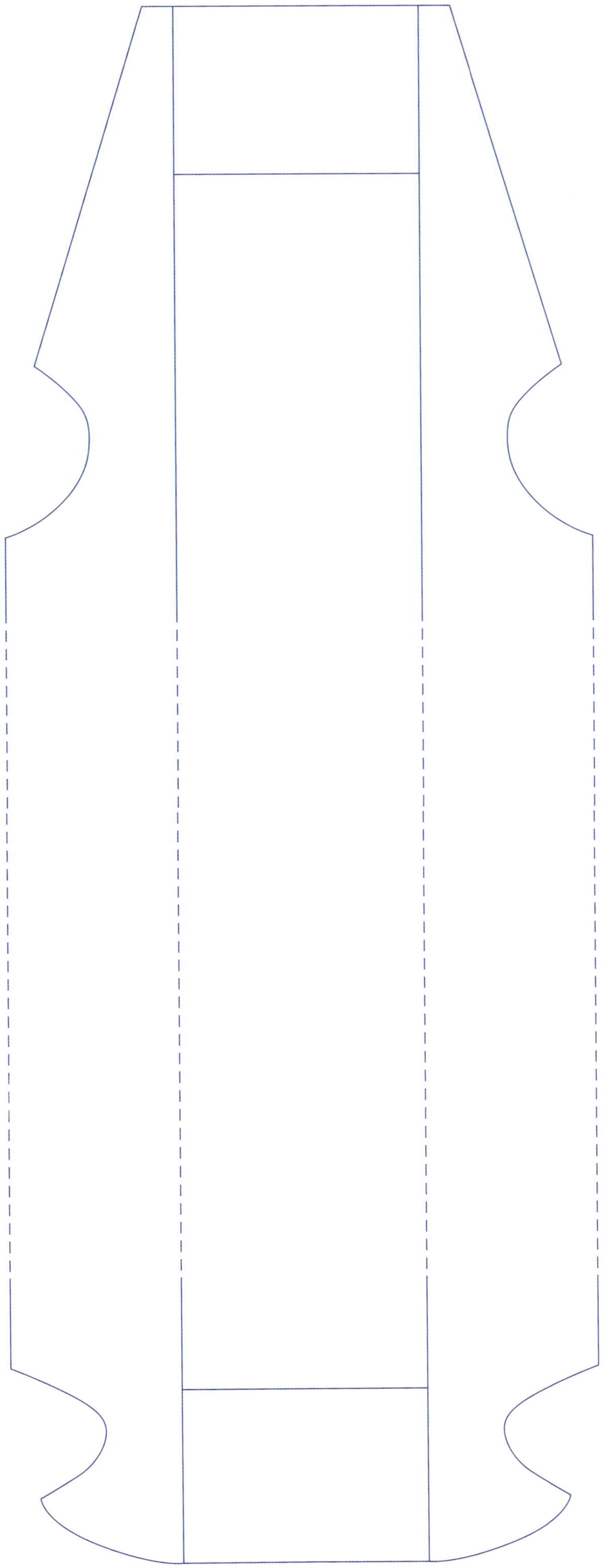

To make the Willow and Hazel Pig featured on pages 218–221, you will need to enlarge the template above by 250%. It is recommended that you use the template for the head and rear of the pig only. The dotted lines serve to represent the actual length of the pig measured from the front to the back legs. This measurement should be 45cm (18in). The distance between the two pieces of wood should be 10cm (4in).

Suppliers

UNITED KINGDOM

Aldershaw Handmade
Tiles Ltd
Tel: 01424 756777
Fax: 01424 756888
tiles@aldershaw.co.uk
www.aldershaw.co.uk
Terracotta, ceramic and brick.

Anthemion Ltd
Tel and Fax: 0208 943 4000
info@ornamentalantiques.com
www.ornamentalantiques.com
Antique garden ornaments.

Brampton Willows
Tel: 01502 575891
Fax: 01502 575890
robertyates@bramptonwillows.
fsnet.co.uk
www.bramptonwillows.co.uk
Willow structures.

Burlington Slate Ltd
Tel: 01229 889 661
Fax: 01229 889 466
sales@burlingtonstone.co.uk
www.burlingtonslate.co.uk
Slate.

Gaze Burvill UK
Tel: 020 7471 8500
Fax: 01420 587354
webenquiries@gazeburvil.com
www.gazeburvill.com
Oak furniture.

CED Ltd (Head Office)
Tel: 01708 867237
Fax: 01708 867 230
sales@ced.ltd.uk
www.ced.ltd.uk
Pebbles, gravel and boulders. Local depots and mail order.

Tom Clark Gallery
Tel: 01935 822833
Fax: 01935 824455
tom@tomclarkstonecarver.co.uk
www.tomclarkstonecarver.co.uk
Stone carving and sculpture.

Compass Glass Ltd
Tel: 020 8946 8080
Fax: 020 8879 0888
www.compassglass.co.uk
Glass.

S & B Evans & Sons Ltd.
Tel: 0207 729 6635
Fax: 0207 613 3558
mail@sandbevansandsons.com
www.sandbevansandsons.com
By appointment. Terracotta.

Dennis Fairweather
Tel and Fax: 01379 852266
info@fairweathersculpture.com
www.fairweathersculpture.com
Bronze resin sculpture, by appointment.

Fantails
Tel: 01929 427676
Fax: 01929 421509
info@fantails.net
www.fantails.net
Garden swings and Adirondack furniture.

Fire and Iron Gallery
Tel: 01372 386453
Lucy@fireandiron.co.uk
www.fireandiron.co.uk
Ironwork and sculpture.

Fired Earth
Tel: 01295 812088
Fax: 01295 810832
enquiries@firedearth.com
www.firedearth.com
Tiles.

Forgetec Engineering
Tel: 01594 835363
Fax: 01594 835363
Metals.

Forsham Cottage Arks
Robert and Cindy Pellett
Tel: 01233 820229
Fax: 01233 820157
office@forshamcottagearks.com
www.forshamcottagearks.com
Dovecotes, poultry housing, waterfowl aviaries.

Full Blown Metals Ltd
Tel: 0709 212 6874
enquiries@stephennewby.co.uk
www.fullblownmetals.com
Metals.

David Harber Sundials Ltd
Tel: 01491 576956
Fax: 01491 413524
sales@davidharbersundials.co.uk
www.davidharbersundials.co.uk
Sundials and sculpture.

Ibstock Brick Ltd
Tel: 0870 903 4000
Fax: 01530 257457
marketing@ibstock.co.uk
www.ibstock.com
Tiles.

Jaymart Rubber & Plastics Ltd
Tel: 01373 864926
Fax: 01373 858454
matting@jaymart.net
www.jaymart.net
Astroturf and rubber matting.

Therese Lang, TJM Associates,
Tel: 01373 812223
festival@tjmassociates.com
www.tjmassociates.com
www.festivalofthegarden.com
International Festival of the Garden (UK).

LASSCO
Tel: 020 7749 9944
Fax: 020 7749 9941
st.michaels@lassco.co.uk
www.lassco.co.uk
Architectural antiques.

Le Blanc Fine Art Foundry
(Lizzard Fountains)
Tel: 01572 787503
Fax: 01572 787688
sculptures@leblancfineart.com
www.leblancfineart.com
Bronze fountains and sculpture.

Lightscape Projects
Tel: 020 7231 5323
Fax: 020 7237 4342
Glass.

The Lister Lutyens
Company Ltd
Tel: 01323 431177
Fax: 01323 639314
sales@listerteak.com
www.listerteak.com
Outdoor leisure furniture.

Luxcrete Ltd
Tel: 020 8965 7292
Fax: 020 8961 6337
sales@luxcrete.co.uk
www.luxcrete.co.uk
Glass.

Marko Polo Designs
Tel: 07973 711049
info@marko-polo.co.uk
www.marko-polo.co.uk
Furniture and barbecues.

Marshalls Mono Ltd
Tel: 01422 312000
www.marshalls.co.uk
Paving, walls and greenhouses.

Christopher Marvell
Tel: 01223 880444
www.christopher@
christopher marvell.com
www.christophermarvell.com
Sculpture.

Louis Poulsen (UK) Ltd
Outdoor Lighting Div
Tel: 01372 848800
Fax: 01372 848801
info@olf.co.uk
www.louis.poulsen.co.uk
Glass.

Reads Nursery
Norfolk NR14 6QW
Tel: 01508 548395
Fax: 01508 548040
sales@readsnursery.co.uk
www.readsnursery.co.uk
Plants, by catalogue and mail order.

Redwood Stone
Tel: 01749 677777
Fax: 01749 671177
sales@redwoodstone.com
www.redwoodstone.com
Stone ornament.

Rimex Metals (UK) Ltd
Tel: 020 8804 0633
Fax: 020 8804 7275
sales@rimexmetals.com
www.rimexmetals.com
Metals.

The Romantic Garden Nursery
Tel: 01603 261488
Fax: 01603 864231
enquiries@romantic-garden-nursery.co.uk
www.romantic-garden-nursery.co.uk
Topiary and plants.

RTC Safety Surfaces
Tel: 01282 414131
Fax:01282 414133
sales@rtcsafety.co.uk
www.rtcsafety.co.uk
Rubber.

Helen Sinclair
Sculpture Culture
Tel: 01792 390 798
Fax: 01792 390 004
helen@sculptureculture.co.uk
www.sculptureculture.co.uk
Sculpture.

Solopark plc
Tel: 01223 834663
Fax: 01223 834780
info@solopark.co.uk
www.solopark.co.uk
Traditional period building materials and supplies.

Thermalite
Tel: 08705 258258
Fax: 01234 762040
info.buildingproducts@hanson.biz
www.thermalite.co.uk
Concrete.

Town and Country Paving
Tel: 01903 776297
Concrete paving.

Zinc Counters
Tel and Fax: 01765 677808
sales@zinccounters.co.uk
www.zinccounters.co.uk
Metals.

BELGIUM

Luc D'Hulst
Tel: 32 (0)3 484 60 72
Fax: 32 (0)3 484 61 31
info@lucdhulst.be
www.lucdhulst.com
Wood.

FRANCE

Joan Clifton Garden Design
La Bailesse
81440 Vénès
Tel: 0033 5 63 70 71 38
la-bailesse@wanadoo.fr
www.la-bailesse.com
By appointment. Architectural ornament, planters, garden furniture. Design consultancy.

Compact Concrete
Tel: 0033 (0) 1 46 71 90 88
Fax: 0033 (0) 1 46 70 99 56
www.compactconcrete.com
Furniture.

AUSTRALIA

Cotswold Garden Furniture
Tel: (02) 9906 3686
Furniture.

Jardinique Pty Ltd
Tel: (02) 9908 7000
Landscape design and construction.

Parterre Garden
Tel: (02) 9363 5874
Fax: (02) 9327 8466
Garden design and furniture.

Porter's Original Paints
Tel: (02) 9698 2017
www.porterspaints.com
Paints. Distributed in all states.

Whitehouse Gardens
Tel: (03) 9877 1430
www.whitehousegardens.com.au
Garden ornaments.

NEW ZEALAND

Auckland Glass
Tel: 09415 8995
auckland.glass@xtra.co.nz
www.aucklandglass.co.nz
Glass.

Capital Stone Ltd
Tel: (09) 443 1031
Marble and granite.

Firth
Tel: 0800 800 576
Fax: 0800 800 530
info@firth.co.nz
www.firth.co.nz
Concrete, bricks and paving.

Winstone Glass
Tel: (09) 444 2797
Fax: (09) 444 2795
www.winstoneglass.com
Glass.

UNITED STATES

Bear Creek Lumber
Tel: 800 597-7191
Fax: 509 997-2040
customerservice@bearcreeklumber.com
www.bearcreeklumber.com
Timber.

Garden Oaks Specialties
Tel: (800) 590-7433
gardenoaks@aol.com
www.gardenoaks.com
Furniture.

Gardener's Supply Company
Tel: (800) 833-1412
Fax: (800) 551-6712
www.gardeners.com
Garden supplies.

High Plains Stone
Tel: (303) 791-1862
Fax: (303) 791-1919
www.highplainsstone.com
Stone.

The Home Depot
Tel: (800) 430-3376
www.homedepot.com
Garden supplies.

Lowe's
www.lowes.com
Garden furniture and supplies.

Plant Delights Nursery, Inc
Tel: (919) 772-4794
Fax: (919) 662-0370
office@plantdelights.com
www.plantdelights.com
Unusual perennials.

Index

Page numbers in *italics* refer to illustrations.

Acknowledgements

The publishers would like to thank the following garden owners, designers and institutions for allowing their gardens to be photographed for this book. All photographs were taken by Jo Whitworth, unless stated otherwise.

t = top b = bottom c = centre
l = left r = right

Amberley Japanese Garden, nr. Beaworthy, Devon 64r; 65r
Baggy House (architects: Hudson Featherstone, London) 78t; 192bl; 193bl
Brook Hall (designers: Prof. Keith Hopkins and Dr. Jennifer Hopkins) 44r; 21bl; 23cr; 49tr; 183cl
Chelsea Flower Show, 1999, 16 ('The Sensory Garden'/designer: Claire Whitehouse); 21tl ('Horti-Couture'/ designer: James Alexander-Sinclair); 22 and 23cl (bottom) ('Help the Aged World Life Garden'/designer: Naila Green); 23tr; 28r; 34 l and c ('Sculpture in the Garden'/designer: George Carter); 44l 'My Retreat'/designer: Andrew Bond); 63tc (photographer: Jonathan Buckley); 72 ('A Floating Garden'/designer: Paul Cooper); 75tr ('The Daily Telegraph Reflective Garden'/ designer: Michael Baston); 78b (photographer: Jonathan Buckley); 169b (Courtyard Garden, Pembrokeshire Horticultural Society); 169b (Courtyard Garden, Pembrokeshire Horticultural Society); 175t ('Help the Aged World Life Garden'/designer: Naila Green); 192tl ('Mr. McGregor's Garden'/designer: Jacquie Gordon); 192br ('21st Century Street'/ designer: Carol Klein); 193tr (Selsdon & District Horticultural Society); 193br 'My Retreat'/ designer: Andrew Bond); 202br (photographer: Jonathan Buckley); 203b (photographer: Jonathan Buckley); 204 ('The Chef's Roof Garden/designer: Terence Conran); 214t (photographer: Jonathan Buckley); 216tl (photographer: Jonathan Buckley); 217tr (photographer: Jonathan Buckley); 234l (photographer: Jonathan Buckley); 235r; 243t (photographer: Jonathan Buckley); 245r ('Mr McGregor's Garden'/
designer: Jacquie Gordon)
The Coppice, Reigate, Surrey 183cr (photographer: Jonathan Buckley)
East Ruston Old Vicarage, Norwich 37b; 38l; 39bl; 168bl; 173t; 177c; 192tr; 241r
Forge Cottage, Jaspers Green (designer: Carolynn Blythe) 20; 21bc; 23bl; 29tl; 48tl; 68tl; 169tr; 172tr
Fairweather Sculpture, Hillside House, Startston, Norfolk (garden designer and sculptor: Dennis Fairweather) 216tr; 217tl and tc; 234l
Fovant Hut, Wiltshire (designer: Christina Oates) 48br; 71tr; 173cl; 17t; 177r
The Garden in Mind, Hampshire (designer: Ivan Hicks) 9l; 9c; 63tl; 222b; 223t; 234r; 235c
Will Giles, Oak Tree House, Norwich 191b; 243cr
Hampton Court Flower Show, 1999 13l, 21tc and 23cl (top) ('Anglo Aquarium Plant Garden', designer: Jane Sweetser); 23tl; 25c ('Feng Shui Garden'/sculptor: Janis Ridley); 45 ('Feng Shui Garden' /designer: Pamela Woods); 64t (sculptor: Dennis Fairweather); 182t ('A Safe Haven Garden'/designer: Ruth Chivers); 203cr ('A Safe Haven Garden'/ designer: Ruth Chivers); 205c (Beachcomber Trading Ltd. Herts.); 244t ('Merlin's Water Garden'/designer: Graham Robb); 244c ('A Safe Haven Garden'/ designer: Ruth Chivers); 245t ('Merlin's Water Garden'/designer: Graham Robb); 245bl; 250 ('Anglo Aquarium Plant Garden'/designer: Jane Sweetser)
The Hannah Peschar Sculpture Garden, Black and White Cottage, Ockley, Surrey (designed by Anthony Paul, Landscape Designer) 11cl (bottom) and 14t ('Winged Arch' by Stephanie Burn); 13bc (wood-carving in oak by Walter Bailey); 24 ('Amongst Words and Phrases' by Mark Clayne Frith); 25l; 62t ('Sit' by Hannah Peschar); 62b (bridge designed by Anthony Paul); 168br and 229l ('Vein II' by Lucien Simon); 176l (reclaimed steps by Anthony Paul); 190cr (deck designed by Antony Paul/stoneware by Jennifer Jones); 193tl; 202br; 222t ('Pictish Spiral Bench' by Nigel Ross); 223b ('Trunks' by Giles Kent); 228c ('Organic Form' by Peter Clarke'); 228r ('King and Queen' by Helen Sinclair); 229c and 229r ('Euridice' by Helen Sinclair); 242t ('Swaylines' by Andrew Ewing)
Heale House Garden, Middle Woodford, nr. Salisbury SP4 6NT, tel: 91722 782504 (open to the public) 23tc; 29tc; 40l, 63tr; 63cl; 205r; 202bl
Hillbarn House, Great Bedwyn, Wiltshire 49tl; 177b
Iford Manor, Bradford-on-Avon, Wiltshire 15br; 23br; 28c; 32; 33; 39r; 60b; 168t; 214c; 214b; 215cr; 216tc; 242b; 243cl
Le Manoir aux Quat' Saisons, Oxon 49br; 61b; 182c; 216b; 242c
Little Cottage, Lymington 169tc; 244bl
The New Art Centre Sculpture Park & Gallery, Roche Court, nr. Salisbury, Wiltshire 180t ('Moonstone III' by Meical Watts); 180b ('Inceptis Gravibus' by Brenda Berman and Annet Stirling); 181tl ('Initial Posts' by Martin Jennings); 181tr ('Found Letter's by Alex Peever); 181bl ('Hermetic Numerals' by John Das Gupta); 181br ('WB Yeats Table' by James Salisbury); 228l ('Butterfly Gate' by Victoria Rance)
Osler Road, Oxford (designers: Mr. and Mrs. N. Coote) 178l and r; 42; 179tl and bl; 202t
Painswick Rococco Garden, Painswick, Glos 36t
RHS Gardens, Wisley 28t
Starston Hall, Norfolk (designer: Christina Baxter) 11br; 21br; 172bl
St. Regis Close, London N10 (designers: S. Bennett and E. Hyde/ garden is open under National Gardens Scheme) 190b
Tatton Park, RHS Flower Show, 1999 ('Oasis in the Urban Jungle'/designer: Jan Williams) 79r
Julia van den Bosch's garden, Ham, London 17l; 27t; 190t; 251
West Green House Garden, near Hartney Wintney, Hampshire 7b; 11lb; 18r; 183b; 185b; 205l; 240t (garden owner and designer: Marylynn Abbott).
Gay Wilson (garden designer) 33
Balmuir Gardens, Putney, London 18bl; 172c; 190cl; 191t
Diana Yakeley (garden designer), 13 College Cross, Islington, London 9r; 11tr; 30c; 35r; 169tl; 191cr; 203t

The publishers would also like to thank the following picture agencies and photographers for allowing their images to be reproduced for this book:

EWA = Elizabeth Whiting Associates

GPL = The Garden Picture Library

2 (Steven Wooster); 3tl EWA (Beckley Park, Oxon); 6 EWA; 7t Houses & Interiors (Steve Sparrow); 7c GPL (Steven Wooster); 8 EWA; 10t EWA; 10b GTRE/ John Glover (Tresco Abbey Gardens, Isles of Scilly); 11tl EWA; 11lc (top) EWA (Beckley Park, Oxon); 12 EWA; 13r GPL (Christopher Gallagher); 14b Bruce Coleman Collection/Derek Croucher (Chateau Chenonceau, France); 15t Wildlife Matters (The Blue Steps, Naumkeag, Massachusetts, USA/designer:

Fletcher Steele); 15bl GPL (Ron Evans); 15bc Houses & Interiors (Mark Bolton); 17c Chelsea Flower Show, 1997 (Yves St Laurent Garden/designer: Madison Cox); 17r GPL (JS Sira); 18tl Jonathan Buckley (designer: Anthony Noel); 19 GPL (Michael Paul); 25r Bruce Coleman Collection (Kim Taylor); 26t Jonathan Buckley (Pashley Manor, Sussex); 26b GPL (Steven Wooster); 27b A–Z Botanical Collection Ltd. (Darryl Sweetland); 28bl Jonathan Buckley (Church Lane, London/designer: PaulKelly); 29tr Sutton Place, Guildford, Surrey; 29b A–Z Botanical Collection Ltd. (Derrick Ditchburn); 30t Wildlife Matters (S. California, USA/designer: Isabelle Green); 30b GDJ/John Glover (Derek Jarman's garden, Kent); 31 EWA (La Mortella, Italy); 36b GPL/JS Sira (Ham House, Surrey); 36c GPL (Henk Dijkman); 37t GPL (Ron Sutherland); 38t GPL (Howard Rice); 40tr GPL (Ron Sutherland); 40br EWA p238 © Steven Wooster/John Gosney; 42 EWA; 43 GPL (Clay Perry); 44c EWA; 46 GPL/Brigitte Thomas (Villandry, France); 47t GPL/John Glover (Hadspen House, Somerset); 47c GPL/John Glover (Preen Manor, Shropshire); 47 Houses & Interiors (Mark Bolton); 48bl GPL (Claire Davies); 50 EWA; 51 EWA; 52t EWA; 52c GPL (Roger Hyam); 52b EWA; 53t GPL (Roger Hyam); 53c EWA; 53b EWA; 54tl EWA; 54bl Houses & Interiors (Steve Sparrow); 54r EWA; 55t EWA; 55b EWA; 56t EWA; 56b EWA; 57 EWA; 58 EWA; 59 GPL (John Glover); 60t Houses & Interiors (Sandra Ireland); 61t EWA; 63c EWA; 63bc EWA (The Water Gardens, Kingston Hill); 67 EWA; 68tc Garden & Wildlife Matters (Derek Jarman's garden, Kent); 68b GDS/John Glover (Derek Jarman's garden, Kent); 69tr Garden Exposures Picture Library (Andrea Jones); 69b GDS/John Glover (Derek Jarman's garden, Kent); 70tl Simon

Kenny/Belle/Arcaid (Rottnest Island, Australia/designer: Larry Eastwood); 70r GPL (Jerry Pavia); 71br Simon Kenny/Belle/Arcaid (Rottnest Island, Australia/designer: Larry Eastwood); 66 and 70bl (Spike Powell, © Anness Publishing Ltd.); 73 Jonathan Buckley; 74tl, 70tl Simon Kenny/Belle/Arcaid (designer: Garth Barnett); 74bl GPL (Gil Hanly); 74c GPL/Steven Wooster (Chelsea Flower Show, 1999); 75br GPL (Ron Sutherland); 76tl EWA; 76l Garden & Wildlife Matters ('Cognoscenti Garden', Hampton Court Flower Show, 1996/designed by Duncan Heather); 76bl Geoff Lung/Arcaid (Sydney, Australia/architect: Luigi Rosselli); 76r Nicholas Kane/Arcaid (designers: Robert Sakula and Cany Ash); 77 GPL/Steven Wooster (designer: Michelle Osborne); 82 Chelsea Flower Show 2003/Eric de Maier and Jane Hudson (designer); 83b ('The Wrong Garden' Chelsea Flower Show 2003/James Dyson and Tim Honey (designers); 84 © Steven Wooster/Luciano Giubbilei (designer); 86t Hampton Court Flower Show (2003)/May & Watts Garden Design (designer); 88 © Steven Wooster; 89 Chelsea Flower Show (2003)/Tom Stuart-Smith (designer); 90t © Steven Wooster/Luciano Giubbilei (designer); 91 'Garden from the Desert', Chelsea Flower Show (2003)/Christopher Bradley-Hole (designer); 92t and b Chelsea Flower Show (2003)/Eric de Maeijer & Jane Hudson (designers); 94t 'Sensuality', Chelsea Flower Show 2003; 94b Latchetts, UK; 95 Chaumont Garden Festival 2003; 96t Westonbirt Festival of the Garden 2003; 96b Ted Smyth (designer); 97 Luciano Giubbilei (designer); 98 Tatton Park Flower Show 2003/Robert Frier at Charlesworth Design (designer); 101 Bowles & Wyer (designers); 103t Chaumont Garden Festival 2003; 103b Chelsea Flower Show; 105 Bowles & Wyer (designer); 108 © Steven Wooster/Chelsea Flower Show 1998; 109 'Sanctuary', Tatton Park Flower Show 2003/Jane Mooney (designer); 112 © Steven Wooster/'The Living Sculpture Garden', Chelsea Flower Show 2000/Christopher Bradley-Hole (designer); © Steven Wooster/Josie Martin (owner); 112l Tatton Park Flower Show 2003; 112r Tatton Park Flower Show 2003; 113b © Steven Wooster/Annie Wilkes (designer); 116 © Steven Wooster; 117 Tatton Park Flower Show 2003; 118t Tatton Park Flower Show 2003; 118b Chaumont Festival of the Garden 2003; 119 Chaumont Garden Festival; 120 © Steven Wooster; 121l © Steven Wooster; 121r © Steven Wooster/Ted Smyth (designer); 122l Chelsea Flower Show 2003; 122r Westonbirt Festival of the Garden 2003; 123 Chelsea Flower Show 2003; 124t © Jenny Hendy/'Flanade'; 124b © Steven Wooster; 125 © Steven Wooster/'Entre Ciel et Terre', Chaumont Garden Festival/Vincent Mayot & Thierry Nenot (designer); 126t © Garden Picture Library (Gary Rogers)/ 'Mother Earth', Chelsea Flower Show 2001/Ian Taylor (designer); 126b 'The Old and the New', Chelsea Flower Show 2003/Pickard School of Garden Design design; 127 © Steven Wooster/ Luciano Giubbilei (designer); 128 Westonbirt Festival of the Garden 2003; 129 Chelsea Flower Show 2003; 130 © Steven Wooster/ Rod Barrett & David Mitchell (designer); 131l © Steven Wooster; 131r Ted Smyth (designer); 132 Westonbirt Festival of the Garden 2003; 133 © Steven Wooster/Tim Feather Design (designer); 134t and b Chaumont Garden Festival 2003;135l 'An Archeologist's Urban Retreat', Hampton Court Flower Show 2003/Sarah Lloyd (design); 135r Arley Hall, Cheshire; 136l Interart Gallery, Holland; 136r Chelsea Flower Show 2003; 137 Tatton Park Flower Show 2003/Aedas, Mary Hoult & Ann Picot (designer); 138 Chelsea Flower Show 2003; 139 Wyken Hall, UK; 140t © Steven Wooster/Scutt's garden, New Zealand; 140b © Steven Wooster/Halmer Searle & Alan Bettesworth; 141 © Steven Wooster/Ross & Paula Greenville; 142 © Steven Wooster/Ross & Paula Greenville; 143t © Steven Wooster; 143b © Steven Wooster; 'Diamond Garden'/Bowles & Wyer (designer); 145t Chelsea Flower Show 2003; 145b 'Al Fresco Living', Tatton Park Flower Show 2003/Xternal Dimensions (designer); 146b © Jenny Hendy; 207t and b Luciano Giubbilei (designer); 148 Chaumont Garden Festival 2003; 149 Westonbirt Festival of the Garden 2003; 150 Westonbirt Festival of the Garden 2003; 151t Chaumont Garden Festival 2003; 151b © Jenny Hendy/Ellerslie Flower Show 2002; 153 Westonbirt Festival of the Garden 2003; 154 Chaumont Garden Festival 2003; 157 Chaumont Garden Festival 2003; 159 Chaumont Garden Festival 2003; 160 © Jenny Hendy; 161 Ellerslie Flower Show 2003; 163t Chaumont Garden Festival 2003; 163bl © Steven Wooster/'The Observatory', Chaumont Garden Festival/Philip Brown & Martin Lonsdale (designer); 163br Westonbirt Festival of the Garden 2003; 165 Westonbirt Festival of the Garden2003; 166 'The Chattel House Garden', Chelsea Flower Show 2003/Murdoch Wickham (designer); 170bl GPL/Ron Sutherland (designer: Anthony Paul); 170c S & O Mathews (Conholt Park); 171tr EWA; 172br GPL (Lamontagne); 173cr GPL (Eric Crichton); 173b EWA; 174b GPL (Howard Rice); 175b Houses & Interiors (Sarah Ireland); 176r EWA; 177t EWA; 179tr and 179bc Jonathan Buckley (Lyndhurst Square, London/Josephine Pickett-Baker (designer); 179br Jonathan Buckley (16 Prospect Road, Warwickshire); 182b S & O Mathews; 184 S &O Mathews (Old Place Farm); 190b Chelsea Flower Show 2003; 191cl Garden & Wildlife Matters (bench designer: Gaze Burvill); 193tl Maria Ornberg (designer); 195bl Ted Smyth (designer); 195br ('The Harbour Garden' Chelsea Flower Show 2003/Michelle Brown (designer); 202br Jonathan Buckley; 206br Bowley & Wyer (designer); 215t GPL (Juliette Wade); 224tr Interart Gallery; 224bl © Steven Wooster/Chaumont Garden Festival 2001; 225bt Westonbirt Festival of the Garden 2003; 226 Interart Gallery, Holland; 227r Chelsea Flower Show 2003/Mark Gregory (designer); 234l see trannie 5; 240l GPL (Michael Howes); 240b EWA; 241t GPL (John Glover); 239b Chelsea Flower Show 2003; 240 Bowles & Wyer (designers).

The publishers would also like to thank the following for their contributions to this book: Thérèse Lang, Bettina and Francesco Passaniti at Compact Concrete (www.compactconcrete.com) and John Wyer of Bowles & Wyer.

PROJECT CONTRIBUTORS

Rosie Brister
Speckled Hen Cottage
27 Chapel Street, Stoke-by-Clare
Tel: 01787 278932
Willow and Hazel Pig (pp.218–21) and Willow Obelisk (pp.186–9)

George Carter
Silverstone Farm
North Elmham, Norfolk
NR20 5EX
Tel: 01362 668130
Metal-Trimmed Planter (pp.210–13)

Ivan Hicks
Garden House
Stanstead Park, Rowland's Castle
Hampshire PO9 6DX
Tel: 01705 413149
Cloud Topiary (pp.236–9)

John Libert
End Cottage, 66 Old Road
Wateringbury, Kent
Tel: 01622 820595
Metal Mobile (pp.230–3)

Ben Pike
Round Trees, Smallway
Congresbury
North Somerset
BS49 6AA
Tel: 01934 876355
Steel Water Feature (pp.246–7)

Mary Rawlinson
1 Bower Gardens
Salisbury
Wiltshire SP1 2RL
Tel: 01722 321745
Tree Seat (pp.196–7)

Tabby Riley
15 Dumont Road
London N16 ONR
Tel: 020 7241 6629
Painted Pots (pp.208–9) and Mosaic Table (pp.198–201)